ANTONY BASHIR: METROPOLITAN & MISSIONARY

St Vladimir's Seminary Press

ORTHODOX CHRISTAN PROFILES SERIES

Number 3

The Orthodox Christian Profiles Series acquaints the reader on an intimate level with Orthodox figures that have shaped the direction of the Orthodox Church in areas of mission, ascetical and liturgical theology, scholarly and pastoral endeavors, and various other professional disciplines. The people featured in the series are mostly our contemporaries and most remain active in shaping the life of the Church today. A few will have fallen asleep in the Lord, but their influence remains strong and worthy of historical record. The mission of this series is to introduce inspirational Orthodox Christian leaders in various ministries and callings that build up the Body of Christ.

Chad Hatfield
Series Editor

Antony Bashir

METROPOLITAN

&

MISSIONARY

Constantine Nasr

ST VLADIMIR'S SEMINARY PRESS
YONKERS, NEW YORK
2012

Library of Congress Cataloging-in-Publication Data

Nasr, Constantine.
  Antony Bashir : metropolitan & missionary / Constantine Nasr.
    p. cm. — (Orthodox Christian profiles series ; no. 3)
  Includes bibliographical references (p.   ) and index.
  ISBN 978-0-88141-406-6 (alk. paper)
    1. Bashir, Antony, 1898-1966. 2. Antiochian Orthodox Christian Archdiocese of
  North America—Biography. 3. Antiochian Orthodox Christian Archdiocese of
  North America—Missions. 4. Orthodox Eastern Church—United States—History.
  I. Title.

  BX738.A759B274 2012
  281.9092—dc23
  [B]
                                                                    2011049962

COPYRIGHT © 2012

ST VLADIMIR'S SEMINARY PRESS
575 Scarsdale Rd, Yonkers, NY 10707
1-800-204-2665
www.svspress.com

ISBN 978-0-88141-406-6

PRINTED IN THE UNITED STATES OF AMERICA

CONTENTS

PART TWO
Personal Remembrances of Metropolitan Antony

Acknowledgments

I first met Metropolitan Antony Bashir when I was in my teens in 1961. Later, when I was a seminarian, this project began while I was attending St Vladimir's Orthodox Theological Seminary in Crestwood, New York. At the suggestion of Fr John Meyendorff, I wrote my thesis on Metropolitan Antony in 1973. For almost forty years I continued my research and continued to revise and expand my original effort. You hold in your hands the conclusion of this lifelong project.

Each passing year since I began my research at the seminary has reinforced my conclusion that Antony Bashir was a unique and gifted man who loved the Church and her people, and who believed strongly in her mission and in her unity. I trust that this book will remind those who knew him just how great Metropolitan Antony's contribution to the Orthodox faith in North America was, and serve to introduce him to a new generation that did not have the honor of knowing him.

I could not have completed this manuscript without the help of many people who lent their particular skills and expertise to the effort. Fr John Meyendorff, in particular, served as my thesis advisor and directed my initial research. Bishop Basil Essey, while we were seminarians together at St Vladimir's, assisted me by transcribing the audiotapes of my interviews with the key people in the life of Antony Bashir. I am especially grateful to those I interviewed: Antony Bashir's sister, Adele Khoury; Archdiocese Board Member Monsour H. Laham; Fr Alexander Schmemann; Archbishop Michael Shaheen; Metropolitan Philip Saliba; and many members of the clergy as well. Special thanks go to Fr Antony Gabriel, who granted me access to his unpublished article on Metropolitan Antony and shared his memories of the late metropolitan. I also thank Kay Lehman who, in addition to her duties as our church secretary, assisted by retyping copies of earlier documents. I can never thank each of these individuals enough.

I am forever indebted to Dn Ezra Ham for assisting me in editing and revising the chapters as I added new research over the years. His willingness to read and re-read the manuscript and his thoughtful suggestions helped me carry the burden of telling Antony Bashir's story. His encouragement made it possible for me to complete my life's work.

I wish also to thank my wife Sharon and our sons, Constantine and Philip, who had to put up with my research and the compilation of information and resources on Antony Bashir.

I am so very grateful to everyone who helped me in this project. To those who have passed on: May your memory be eternal. To the living: May God grant you many years.

Fr Constantine Nasr
Mid-Lent, 2011

PART I

Metropolitan Antony:
His History and Achievements

CHAPTER 1

The Early Arab Christians in America

S ince 1961, I have visited many Antiochian parishes in the United States and Canada. In my conversations with clergy and laity, I have found the story of the Syrian Lebanese immigration to be no different from that of any other national group that has come to North America in search of a new life. Fleeing persecution and the yoke of the Ottoman Empire, they sought freedom and better opportunities in life. Their stories were like many others, differing only in time period, ethnic and cultural background, the old country from which they came, and where they ended up in North America. Young and old, they crossed the seas to the land of milk and honey, where the rumor was that "you could dig in the ground and become a millionaire."

Arab Orthodox Christians Arrive in North America

They came penniless and settled across this vast land as strangers to both a language and a culture. Friend brought friend, son brought father, and cousin brought neighbor as they boarded one of the French Line ships or other steamboats. Challenged by the new frontier, they came, wave after wave, to North America, most of them Christians. Many came as unskilled, but once here they threw themselves into work in the factories, mills, and farms, or they peddled from town to town and village to village, trying to establish an identity on these new shores. They came with a vision to succeed and were excited to face the challenges that lay before them.

They came with something special: their Orthodox faith, a belief in Jesus Christ. They knew how to make the sign of the cross; perhaps they had an icon in their suitcase; they may have remembered hymns from the liturgy or stories from the Bible. They also came with their rich Syrian-Lebanese heritage.

They settled in cities and villages, or on farms. They labored hard and lived the North American way of life. They lived near each other, in their own neighborhoods, thus providing themselves with a sense of protection. And they assisted one another in the way that immigrant groups have ever done.

The first Arab Christian family to come to the United States was Professor Joseph Arbeely, his wife, six children, and his daughter-in-law. They came in 1878 from the village of Arbeen near Damascus.[1] They settled in Manhattan, across the East River. The immigration quota for the Middle East was limited entry. In 1895, however, the Chicago World's Fair drew many from the Middle East. These came in the hope of joining their relatives and friends who were already here.

These immigrant communities provided not only physical support for each other, but spiritual support also. Because of their upbringing and their love for God, they began to affiliate with the Russian Orthodox churches in their neighborhoods, for the sake of their liturgical and sacramental needs. The liturgical services comforted the Arab immigrants. Because the services were in Slavonic, however, there was a void. They had a need to hear the services in their native Arabic. As time passed, Arab immigrants established organizations, formed committees, discussed their ethnic concerns, and sought for solutions. In time it became self-evident that they needed Arabic clergymen to minister to them in their own mother tongue.

The fatherly concern of Patriarch Spyridon of Antioch for his people paved the way for Fr Constantine Tarazy of Damascus to come to the United States. He came in order to visit and evaluate the need for establishing an Antiochian parish here.[2] Excited about this new

---

[1]Gregory Aboud, *The Syrian Antiochian Orthodox Church of America* (unpublished manuscript, 1962), p. 2.

[2]Ibid., p. 3.

assignment, he traveled the East Coast, visiting the flock of Antioch. To his disappointment, however, the Arabic Orthodox community was very small and scattered, and it could not afford to sustain a full-time priest. Disappointed, he reluctantly returned to Syria.

Following Fr Constantine Tarazy, Fr Christopher Jabara came to the United States. He was educated both in the faith and in comparative religions, especially in the Old Testament and the Koran, and he was a charismatic man. Within a short time, he had attracted many to follow him, and they gave him moral and financial support. He soon established a place of worship at the intersection of Cedar and Washington Streets, right in the center of New York City.

The Syrian-Lebanese community had high hopes for a successful mission and spiritual growth. But to their disappointment, Fr Christopher began to teach heresy, preaching that the religions of Christ, of Moses, and of Mohammed were, in reality, one religion. He articulated this teaching to gain financial support. Wherever he went, he espoused his views. This news shocked the faithful who supported him. They remembered the persecution they had known under the Ottomans, as well as the recent massacre between the Druze and the Maronites.

At the Chicago World's Fair in 1895, Fr Christopher preached publicly his new philosophy that the Gospel, the Torah, and the Koran are one Bible.[3] Upon his return to New York City, reaction against him mounted, and he was rejected by the Arab Orthodox community in New York. Having no other recourse, he fled to Egypt that same year.

St Raphael Hawaweeny

The Arabic-speaking Orthodox who went to the Chicago World's Fair observed that other national ethnic groups at the Fair were well organized in the presentation of their faith and culture. The Arabs observed and learned. With determination, they voiced their needs and concerns to one another. As a result, they formed the Syrian Orthodox Benevolent Society in 1895. George Bek Qodsy was the

[3]Nicholaos Nahas, *The Witness of Antioch in North America*, p. 27.

prime mover in creating the society; Dr Ibrahim Arbeely, son of Joseph Arbeely, was elected its first president.

The most important task was to find a house of worship to sustain the spiritual and sacramental life of the community. They sought spiritual refuge under the omophore of the Russian Orthodox Church in America. In time, the community petitioned for the well-respected and much loved Archimandrite Raphael Hawaweeny, who was then teaching Arabic at the Academy of Kazan in Russia, to come to the United States. Dr Ibrahim Arbeely corresponded with Fr Raphael, and encouraged him to accept their invitation to serve the Arabic-speaking Orthodox people in this land. Bishop Nicholas, the Russian Orthodox Bishop of Alaska and all North America, was visiting at that time in St Petersburg. Fr Raphael discussed the matter with him, and chose to accept the invitation. Accompanied by his chanter, Constantine Abou-Adal, he arrived in North America on November 17, 1895. He founded the first Arabic-speaking parish in North America at 77 Washington Street in Lower Manhattan. His ministry began to flourish.

By 1900, several thousand Arab immigrants had moved across the East River into Brooklyn. In 1902, the parish purchased a building at 301–303 Pacific Street in Brooklyn, in the heart of the new Arabic-speaking community. On October 27, 1902, Bishop Tikhon, successor to Bishop Nicholas, consecrated St Nicholas church as the mother church for the Arabic-speaking people. In honor of Czar Nicholas, who had financially supported the Antiochian patriarchate, it was named for the great St Nicholas, the fourth-century wonderworking bishop of Myra.[4]

As immigration increased, more communities were established and more missions formed. The Primate of the Russian Church in North America, Bishop Tikhon, saw a need to consecrate Fr Raphael a bishop, so that he could be his vicar and act as spiritual father of the "Syrian Mission." Raphael's consecration took place on March 12, 1904, at St Nicholas church. He was given the title "Bishop of Brook-

---

[4]St Nicholas Cathedral eventually relocated to 305 State Street, Brooklyn, and is considered the "mother parish" of the Antiochian Archdiocese of North America.

lyn" and St Nicholas church was made his cathedral. He was "the first Orthodox bishop of any nationality to be consecrated in North America."[5] Bishop Raphael served with great dignity and added twenty-four parishes to his mission in the years following. He passed away in the Lord on February 27, 1915, at the age of fifty-four.

Descent into Chaos

With the rise of Communism and the Bolshevik Revolution in Russia in 1917, coupled with the outbreak of World War I, Orthodox unity in North America suffered a serious blow. Ethnic parishes faced the pressure of division. Should they remain under the leadership of the Russian Church, or should they reunite with the leadership in their native countries? Ultimately, unity was shattered within the ethnic jurisdictions as well as between them. "The small Syro-Arabian Mission fell victim to this divisiveness."[6]

Bishops visiting from the Old World put pressure on ethnic parishes to reunite with "the old country." After the death of Bishop Raphael, Arab parishes became particularly vulnerable. The challenge was immense. A decision had to be made, whether to unite with the mother church of Antioch or to remain under the Russian Orthodox Church. Among the bishops who came from the Patriarchate of Antioch as guests of Bishop Raphael was a bishop named Germanos Shehadi, the Metropolitan of Selucia and Baalbak.

With the outbreak of World War I, Bishop Germanos found himself trapped in the United States, unable to return to Syria.[7] Having visited the Syrian Mission churches and having been befriended by many who had migrated from his archdiocese in Lebanon and now lived here, he planted a seed by urging the Syrian Mission to move

[5]"The Self-Ruled Antiochian Orthodox Christian Archdiocese of North America: A Brief History." The Self-Ruled Antiochian Orthodox Christian Archdiocese of North America 2011 Directory (Englewood, NJ: 2011), 3.

[6]Aboud, *The Syrian Antiochian Orthodox Church*, 5.

[7]Stephen Upson, "History of the Antiochian Orthodox Christian Archdiocese of All New York and North America," *The 25th Antiochian Orthodox Archdiocese Convention* (Chicago:1970), 20.

under the authority of the Patriarchate of Antioch. It is possible that Bishop Germanos hoped to succeed Bishop Raphael.[8]

Archbishop Evdokim, well aware of this challenge, knew there was a real spiritual void, for there was no Arab bishop to shepherd the flock of Antioch in America. He decided to consecrate Archimandrite Aftimios Ofiesh, who was a priest serving in a Syrian mission in Montreal, Canada, and make him his auxiliary. He would be the immediate successor to the late Bishop Raphael as Bishop of Brooklyn. On May 13, 1917, Ofiesh was duly consecrated. Bishop Aftimios energetically continued the work begun by Raphael with the twenty-eight parishes in the jurisdiction of the Syrian Mission of the Russian Orthodox Church.

Following the end of the First World War and with the changing political climate brought on by the Bolsheviks in Russia, Metropolitan Platon, successor to Archbishop Tikhon of the Russian Orthodox Church of North America, severed his ties with the Moscow Patriarchate. By 1925, he had decided to create an autonomous (self-governing) church out of the Syrian Mission, with Aftimios as its archbishop.

On February 2, 1927, Metropolitan Platon, with his bishops, issued a letter that stated in part:

> We do hereby permit, empower, authorize, and direct the said Archbishop of Brooklyn to found, organize, establish, head, conduct, control, and maintain a distinct, independent, and autonomous branch of the Orthodox Catholic Church to be known and legally established and generally recognized as the Holy Eastern Catholic and Apostolic Church in America.[9]

As people emigrated after the First World War and moved to various parts of America, Archbishop Aftimios' ministry required him to travel east and west, north and south. By 1927, he had consecrated two additional bishops: Sophronios (Beshara), for the diocese of Los Angeles, and Emmanuel Abo-Hatab, for the diocese of Montreal.[10]

---

[8]Ibid., 20.
[9]George Zibrinskie, *Orthodox American Church*, 1928, pp. 1–2.
[10]Upson, "History," 20.

Patriarch Gregory Haddad of Antioch, upon learning that the Archbishop of Brooklyn had been authorized to found and oversee an autonomous Church in America, decided to send Metropolitan Zacharia as his personal representative to look into the Arab Orthodox Church in America. In order to claim the Arab Orthodox in America as its own (and so reclaim them from the autonomy given them by the Russian Church in America), he recommended that Archimandrite Victor Abou-Assaley be consecrated a bishop to lead the Antiochian Orthodox Church in North America. This course of action was blessed by the patriarch.

Archbishop Panteleimon of Neopolis, who represented the Patriarchate of Jerusalem, was at that time in the United States, attending the Episcopal Church's national convention in Portland, Oregon. With his assistance, Metropolitan Zacharia, acting as the personal representative of Patriarch Gregory, consecrated Victor Abou-Assaley bishop at St Mary Albanian Orthodox Church in Worcester, Massachusetts.[11]

As if coming to a strange land where they were ignorant of both the language and the culture was not enough for Arab immigrants, they now faced a dizzying succession of ecclesiastical events that proved bewildering, perplexing, and ultimately destructive. One can understand the tensions, confusion, and devotion of the laity who chose to follow Archbishop Aftimios Ofiesh, who was under the Russian Orthodox Archdiocese of North America, as well as of those who chose to follow Archbishop Victor Abou-Assaley, representing the mother church of Antioch. Those in favor of remaining with the Russian Church were called *Russy*, while those who elected to follow Antioch became known as *Antaky*. The Arab Orthodox community in North America was now divided, resulting in a long period of separation among the Arabic-speaking parishes in North America.

The various factions fought for control of the church. By 1934, however, all of the leaders of these factions had died, with the exception of Aftimios Ofiesh. He, however, relinquished his bishopric on April 19, 1933. Into the resulting vacuum the Patriarch of Antioch

---

[11]Upson, "History," 21.

appointed Archimandrite Antony Bashir as the patriarchal vicar in North America. It was hoped that Bashir could help reunite the Arab Orthodox community by bringing them back into the fold of the mother church of Antioch.

CHAPTER 2

Bashir's Early Life

Antony Bashir was born on March 15, 1898, in Douma, Lebanon, the son of Joseph and Zaina Bashir. His family's roots in the Orthodox Church extended back into the shadows of the distant past.[1] He was raised in the mountain country of Greater Syria, where most of the Orthodox people owed their allegiance to the ancient Patriarchate of Antioch. This holy see, with its triple apostolic foundation by Saints Peter, Paul, and Barnabas, and its 2,000 years of unbroken history, is recognized as one of the oldest in Christendom. It was in Antioch that the followers of Jesus were first called Christians.[2]

Douma—a predominately Orthodox village that also contained a few Maronites and Muslims—was perched high in the mountains of Lebanon. The Bashir family was small. Bashir's father was not considered a rich man; he supported his family by working as a gunsmith. The family gained other income by opening their home as the village guesthouse. Thanks to the variety of guests who stayed in their home, young Antony came into contact with people of all faiths.[3]

Praying for her Children

The family name *Bashir* means "annunciation" or "good news," but Zaina's loss of three children in infancy seemed to mock the name. In

[1] Sam E. Salem, *Metropolitan Antony Bashir: An Appreciation* (Cleveland, OH: 1961), 10.

[2] Acts 11.26.

[3] From a personal interview with Adele Khoury, sister of Antony Bashir, in Brooklyn, NY, March 22, 1971.

19

due time, God blessed the couple with a son, Sabah, and a daughter, Adele. Zaina Bashir, driven to fill the void of her three lost children, made constant pilgrimages to the Orthodox shrines in Douma and the surrounding area, offering prayers and supplications and beseeching God for another child. She prayed most frequently at the church in the monastery of St Antony the Great near Douma. She vowed that, if God should give her another child, she would dedicate him to St Antony. A son was indeed born a year later, on March 15, 1898, and she named him Antony. His great uncle, Fr Elias Khoury, baptized him in the Church of the Theotokos in Douma.[4]

His sister Adele described Antony as "an unusually intelligent and active boy, an old man when he was perhaps sixteen years old."[5] Antony's mind and interests were extremely advanced for his age. He was a natural-born leader and always took the lead in childhood games.

Life under the Ottoman Turks

The Ottoman Turks had conquered Lebanon and made it a part of the Ottoman Empire. Christianity suffered greatly at the hands of the Ottoman Turks. Due to extreme pressure by the Turks, the Ecumenical Patriarch in Constantinople systematically replaced indigenous patriarchs and bishops with fellow Greeks. Over the centuries, these Greek patriarchs lost touch with the indigenous Arabs of the Middle East. Arab Christianity suffered from neglect and a lack of leadership by the Greek bishops. In light of this situation, the Orthodox Church of Russia undertook to strengthen Orthodox Christianity inside the Ottoman Turkish Empire. The Imperial Russian Orthodox Mission sponsored a school in Douma. This school, supported by Russian generosity, was the one that Antony Bashir attended.

In Search of an Education

When Antony was thirteen years old, he left home and enrolled at the Balamand Theological School near Tripoli, in Koura, Lebanon.

[4]Ibid.
[5]Ibid.

Among his teachers was the Archimandrite Ananias Kassab (1888–1971). Little did he and his fellow classmate Samuel David suspect that one day they would both become archbishops, shaping the face of Orthodox Christianity in America. Bashir remained at the Balamand until his ordination to the diaconate on April 16, 1916.

A bright student seeking knowledge, Bashir went on to further his education at the American University of Beirut and the famous Law School of Baabda.[6] He threw himself into his studies, learning the English language and the principles of economics. He filled his notebooks with meticulous notes, writing in English even when the subject was not English. In this way, even as he learned about the relationship between barter economies, money economies, and credit economies, for example, he was also strengthening his English language skills.[7]

Choosing the Priesthood

Antony Bashir loved the Church as much as he loved learning. It is said that Antony's love for the Church came from the influence of his maternal uncle, Elias Ayoub, who was a church chanter, as well as from the great dedication of his immediate family to the Church.[8] The Bashir family was highly respected in the village not only because of their faith, but also for the devotion the parents exhibited toward their children and to each other.[9] Antony's parents permitted him to choose the vocation of the priesthood and, once he had made that decision, did not try to dissuade him from becoming a celibate.

By 1920, Antony Bashir had become known throughout the Arab world as a brilliant young clergyman. He had distinguished himself as secretary to the archbishop of Lebanon and as a teacher at both the American University of Beirut and at Beirut's Zahrat-el-ehson High School. Furthermore, he practiced civil law under such great men as

[6]Salem, *Metropolitan Antony Bashir*, 10.
[7]I wish to thank Adele Khoury for the use of Antony Bashir's notebooks from his days as a student.
[8]Ibid.
[9]Adele Khoury, personal interview.

Najeeb Khalaf, Raji Abou Hyder, and Wakim Iz-el-deen. He also edited and contributed to leading publications such as *The New Women* (*Al-Mara-Aljadida*). This magazine, published by prominent Muslim Julia Tomeh, attempted to improve the position of women in the Muslim world.[10] Antony edited the magazine anonymously.

Give Me Men to Match my Mountains

It was the Church, however, that received the bulk of Antony's energy and attention. Between the years 1915 and 1920, he collaborated with two leading scholars, Archbishop Paul Abou-Adul and Najeeb Khalaf, in compiling what has since earned universal recognition as the most accurate and complete Arabic version of the New Testament.[11] The translation used texts of the Bible in the original Greek, in Russian, and in English, as well as the current Arabic edition. Unfortunately, this Arabic New Testament was never printed, although Khalaf's widow kept the manuscript. In 1956, Metropolitan Antony tried to persuade Mrs Khalaf to give him the translation so that it might be published. However, she vowed to keep the manuscript as a treasured memory of her late husband.[12]

Upon surveying the campus of the American University of Beirut, its founding president had once stated: "Let men come from their mountains . . . to this mountain of learning."[13] Antony Bashir left the mountains surrounding Douma and came to the new mountain of learning in Beirut. In time he grew in stature and became indeed, in both the Old World and the New, a man to match the mountains.

[10]Ibid.
[11]Ibid.
[12]Ibid.
[13]Antony Gabriel. "A Man to Match the Mountains," *The 25th Antiochian Orthodox Archdiocese Convention* (Chicago, IL: 1970).

CHAPTER 3

Arriving in the United States

A fter the fall of Constantinople to the Ottomans in 1453, Christians in the Middle East no longer enjoyed the financial support they had formerly received from the Byzantine Empire. The Russian Patriarchate tried to fill this gap by extending to its sister church in Antioch spiritual and financial support for Christian schools, monasteries, and churches. Then World War I and the Bolshevik Revolution, with the consequent suppression of the Orthodox Church in Russia, brought new financial difficulties to the Antiochian church.[1] In the 1920s, Patriarch Gregory IV of Antioch turned to the United States to find fresh sources of financial support.

Contact with the Episcopal Church in North America

It happened that the Rev. Dr William Emhardt, representing the Episcopal Church in the United States, was on a fact-finding mission in the Middle East at the time, evaluating Episcopalian missionary work in Syria and Lebanon. His subsequent meeting with Patriarch Gregory, Metropolitan Gerasimus Messarah, and Deacon Antony Bashir is described in *The New Herodus*. Published anonymously, the book is widely attributed to Fr Basil Karbawey, secretary to Archbishop Aftimios of Brooklyn.[2] Karbawey's alleged authorship is significant in that *The New Herodus* attempts to reveal the reason why Metropolitan Gerasimus Messarah and his companions came to the United

[1]See "Aftimios Ofiesh," *The Orthodox Catholic Review* 1. 2 (February 1927): 60.

[2]From a personal interview with Rev. Michal Husson. December 28, 1971.

States.[3] Gerasimus' activities in the United States were to have a negative impact upon Archbishop Aftimios and the Arab Christians who remained under the oversight of the Russian Orthodox Church in America.

Shortly after Emhardt's arrival in Syria, Patriarch Gregory IV invited him to come to the Orthodox archdiocesan headquarters in Beirut. Unknown to the Holy Synod, an unofficial meeting between the Patriarch and Emhardt took place, with Deacon Antony Bashir acting as interpreter, at which the hierarch confided to the Rev. Emhardt the serious financial problems facing the Patriarchate of Antioch.[4]

Looking for a Quid Pro Quo

As His Beatitude carefully discussed the financial crisis confronting the Patriarchate of Antioch, Emhardt had his own reasons for listening attentively. Talks with the Bishop of Rome had proved unfruitful in obtaining recognition of the validity of the sacerdotal orders of Episcopalian clergy. Having failed with the Pope, Emhardt now sought out recognition from the Patriarch of Antioch. Emhardt "wished to see the Patriarch of Antioch recognize the validity of the Episcopal Church and its orders. Through this act of recognition, the Episcopal Church would do its best to lift the Antiochian Church out of its period of depression."[5] Emhardt "dangled before the Patriarchate hopes that badly needed charitable monies might become available"[6] should the Holy Synod of Antioch choose to recognize the validity of the Episcopal Church.

Obviously, the Patriarch could not do what Emhardt asked. However, he and Emhardt were careful to leave the door open. Emhardt offered to provide the funds for Patriarch Gregory IV to send a delegation to the general convention of the Episcopal Church, to be held in Portland, Oregon in September of 1922. Seeing an opportunity to

---

[3]Basil Karbawey, *The New Herodus* (USA: 1925), 132.
[4]Ibid., 133.
[5]Ibid.
[6]Ibid.

plead the cause of Antioch, Patriarch Gregory sent Metropolitan Messarah and Deacon Antony Bashir to the United States. However, no promises had been made, no *quid pro quo* agreed to. Emhardt in no way committed himself to the patriarch, nor had Gregory IV pledged himself to the Episcopalian agenda.

Nevertheless, *The New Herodus* quotes the Beirut newspaper, *The Gift*, as follows:

> There will be held in Portland, Oregon, a National Council of Churches to discuss the unity of the Christian denominations. The See of Antioch is sending Metropolitan Messarah as a special representative of Patriarch Gregory. Accompanying him will be Archdeacon Bashir and Victor Abou-Assaley.[7]

According to *The New Herodus,* these delegates kept their meeting with Emhardt a secret. (Even the Syrian Church in America, which was still functioning under the Russian Orthodox Church at the time, did not know about it.) The existence of the delegation and its mission came to light when the brother of Metropolitan Germanos Shehadi, the Metropolitan of Zahle, chanced to run into them in France. He notified by telegram his relatives in Brooklyn of the arrival date of the delegation.[8]

Arriving in the United States

Metropolitan Germanos Shehadi, himself a representative of the Antiochian Church in America since 1916, welcomed the delegation at his residence in Brooklyn. At this time the delegation also visited the Russian Church, where they met Fr Basil Karbawey (the anonymous author of *The New Herodus*), who was the official represent-ative of Archbishop Aftimios of Brooklyn.

During a heated discussion with the hierarchs, the delegation was exposed to the internal splintering and division within the archdiocese. Some Arab parishes remained under Russian oversight, whereas others resented the Russians and wanted to be part of an Arab patri-

[7]Ibid.
[8]Ibid., 135.

archate. Although Metropolitan Germanos and Archbishop Aftimios were shepherding separate flocks under trying circumstances, both hierarchs deeply resented the arrival of Metropolitan Gerasimus Messarah, who became a source of trouble for them. As Fr Karbawey remarked, "Metropolitan Messarah planted a thorn in their hearts."[9]

General Convention of the Episcopal Church

The delegation departed and a few days later arrived at the General Convention of the Episcopal Church in Portland, Oregon, where Archbishop Panteleimon of Neapolis, representing the Patriarchate of Jerusalem, was also present. The *Journal of the General Convention of the Protestant Episcopal Church in the United States* for the year 1922, printed for the Convention of 1923, contained the following resolution adopted at the previous Convention:

> Resolved: That the Chairman of the House of Deputies be requested to supply the Secretary a copy of his remarks introducing the distinguished Greek and Syrian ecclesiastics to this House, and that the Secretary is hereby directed to incorporate such a copy in the minutes of the day.
>
> Your Grace [to Archbishop Panteleimon], it is with sincere gratification that this House of Clerical and Lay Deputies, representing the American Episcopal Church in Convention assembled, gives welcome, through its president, to Your Grace as representing the Patriarch of Jerusalem. This Catholic and Apostolic Communion can never forget Jerusalem, the Mother of All. We rejoice with you that the Crescent in Jerusalem has been supplanted by the Cross, and that the Church, which since the time of Constantine, has had the privilege of guarding the places sacred to all Christendom, where our Lord lived and died and rose again, is now under the protection of a Christian nation. We beg you to convey to the venerable Patriarch of Jerusalem the assurance of our respect and our brotherly good wishes for the peaceful and successful prosecution of his work.

[9]Ibid., 137.

And to Your Grace [turning to His Grace Gerasimus] also, we extend a cordial welcome, representing as you do, the Patriarch of Antioch, in which city the Disciples were first called Christians, reminding us as it does that it was in Antioch that first the Gospel was preached, not only to Jews and proselytes, but to the Gentiles, the beginning of that worldwide missionary movement of the Apostolic Church of which we are the beneficiaries, and we assure him that we are mindful of his request for the fuller cooperation of our own communion in ministering to the Syrians in the United States.[10]

There was no mention of Antony Bashir in the official journal. However, other evidence of his presence is available through photographs taken at the convention. At any rate, Bashir was Metropolitan Gerasimus' personal interpreter.

Looking for Money in America

Following the convention, Gerasimus and Bashir began a tour of Arab communities in the United States, Mexico, and Cuba, seeking aid in the name of Beirut's St George Hospital and School of Peace.[11] The amount that was collected, if indeed any money was collected, is unknown. The significance of the tour lies in the fact that Bashir received, at this time, his first exposure to the divisions in the Church here and the scattered Syrian communities in the United States.

Upon their return to New York, Metropolitan Gerasimus realized he had been unsuccessful in establishing unity within the Syrian-Arab community. In need of funding, Gerasimus sought permanent aid from the Episcopal Church to support Deacon Bashir's continued work among the Syrian Orthodox communities in the United States.[12] Metropolitan Gerasimus and Bashir met with Bishop Gaeler, the Epis-

---

[10]*Journal of the General Convention of the Protestant Episcopal Church* (Portland, Oregon: 1922), 251.

[11]Ibid., 138.

[12]Aftimios Ofiesh, *The Orthodox Catholic Review,* 1. 4–5 (April-May 1927): 151.

copalian bishop in charge of the Foreign-Born Aid Division, to request a monthly salary for Deacon Bashir. This request was met, on the condition that Antony Bashir be ordained a priest and elevated to the administrative rank of Archimandrite.

According to Archbishop Aftimios Ofiesh, who witnessed the meetings in New York City, the Episcopal Church Conference agreed to give "a substantial grant to the [Antiochian] Patriarchate."[13] Later, upon his return to Beirut, Metropolitan Gerasimus Messarah claimed to have received the promise of $150,000 per annum from the Episcopalians.[14] Whether the Patriarchate ever received any money, however, cannot be verified.

In addition to support for the Antiochian Patriarchate, an agreement was also made that Deacon Antony Bashir (secretary to Gerasimus) "should be elevated to the office of archimandrite and designated as the Antiochian envoy to the Episcopal Church in North America. As such, his duties were to encourage the Syrian Orthodox, who had no church of their own, to affiliate with the Episcopal Church, which would make Bashir a monthly allocation of three hundred dollars."[15]

Bashir's Unusual Ordination

Bashir was ordained in 1922 at an Episcopal Church in Atlantic City, New Jersey, by Metropolitan Gerasimus. He was ordained in an Episcopal church in order to please the Episcopalian Bishop Gaeler by demonstrating cooperation between the Episcopal and the Orthodox Churches.[16] The author of *The New Herodus* considered Bashir's ordination "non-canonical," and many Syrians in this country were equally critical.

Archimandrite Antony Bashir began his journeys among the Syrian people in America as a missionary priest under the auspices and

---

[13]Mariam Namey Ofiesh, *Archbishop Aftimios Ofiesh* (Sun City West, AZ: Aftimios Abihider, 1999), 78.
[14]Karbawey, *The New Herodus,* 211.
[15]Mariam Namey Ofiesh, 78.
[16]Karbawey, *The New Herodus,* 148.

salary of the Episcopal Church. The ostensible purpose of Bashir's mission was to approach Arab Christians who had no resident clergy. As noted above, some of the Arab Orthodox in North America were active in Arab parishes under Archbishop Aftimios Ofiesh and the Russians, while others were now under Archbishop Victor Abou-Assaley and the Antiochians. There were still many Orthodox Arabs who did not attend any parish or who lived in areas where no Arab language Orthodox parishes existed. Archimandrite Antony's mission, however, was almost entirely confined to visiting localities within the Syrian mission that were under Russian jurisdiction. While Archbishop Aftimios Ofiesh resisted the incursion of Victor Abou-Assaley and the Antiochians, he suspected that Bashir had been put to work by the Episcopalians to convince any Arab Orthodox who did not live near an Arab Orthodox parish to join their nearby Episcopal parish.

Bashir's work, under the direction of Gerasimus and Emhardt, irritated the faithful of the Syrian mission.[17] Inevitably, the Archdiocese of Brooklyn responded to the protests of loyal Syrians by exposing the entire Protestant Episcopal activities in the Syrian-language newspapers. Ultimately, Bashir's work was unsuccessful, and the Protestant Episcopal National Council discontinued Bashir's salary at the end of the year.[18]

Breaking Formal Ties with the Episcopal Church

Based on records found in the archives of the Episcopal Church, there is no indication that the Church's intentions were anything other than a readiness to assist the Syrian communities in this country. Dr Paul Anderson, an expert on Anglican-Eastern Orthodox relations and a member of the Executive Council of the Episcopal Church, stated (both in a letter and in private conversation) that the purpose of this financial assistance was simply an expression of charity towards the Syrian people in this country.

[17]Aftimios Ofiesh, 151.
[18]Karbawey, *The New Herodus*, 230.

It has been impossible to find documentation of Fr Antony's salary or of his reasons for breaking his ties with the Episcopal Church. It would seem that Fr Antony's only goal was to strengthen the Orthodox faith of Syrian Christians. If the Episcopalians were willing to pay him to do that, then he was willing to let them do so. As for the Episcopal Church, it assisted Fr Antony in the hopes of bringing about closer ecclesiastical ties between the two churches.

This attempt was unsuccessful, however, because Fr Antony was dedicated and devoted to the Orthodox Church and her people. Perhaps the Episcopal Church only sponsored him in hopes that such a gesture would carry weight with Patriarch Gregory of Antioch. However, when it became apparent that supporting Fr Antony would not gain Gregory's support for recognizing the validity of the Episcopal Church and her clergy, funds from the Episcopal Church were discontinued and Fr Antony ceased to be associated with that body.

CHAPTER 4

A Parish Priest

After severing ties with the Episcopal Church, Fr Antony took a leave of absence while he joined his mother and several other members of his family in Chihuahua, Mexico. While there, he spent his time writing and translating. He especially enjoyed translating the works of Khalil Gibran, the most celebrated Lebanese poet of the twentieth century.

After two years of independent work in Mexico, Fr Antony received a call from the newly elected Archbishop Victor Abou-Assaley, who was now governing the Arab Christians in America who were under the Patriarchate of Antioch. He asked Bashir to come and assist him in organizing parishes across the United States. Already well-versed in English and quick to adapt himself to the New World, Fr Antony took on the challenge of traveling the length and breadth of the North American continent, building churches, serving parishes, and organizing societies throughout the United States, Canada, and Mexico.

Terre Haute, Indiana

Fr Antony's work in establishing St George Orthodox Church in Terre Haute, Indiana, is indicative of his labors throughout North America. Mr Woodre G. Corey, a member of the Terre Haute Syrian community, went to Cleveland, Ohio, in 1925 to attend a general convention of the archdiocese.[1] While there, he met Fr Antony and discussed with him the possibility of establishing a parish in Terre Haute. Over the

---

[1]The discussion of the founding of the parish in Terre Haute, Indiana, is taken from a brief history of St. George Orthodox Church that was written by George M. Rados in 1967, on the occasion of the 40*th* anniversary of the parish. George M. Rados, *St. George Orthodox Church: 40th Anniversary* (Terre Haute, ID: 1967).

next two years, as Fr Antony served various parishes in Indianapolis and the Midwest, he stayed in contact with the community in Indiana. By 1927, Fr Antony was ready to move forward with a church in Terre Haute. He invited Mr Corey and a delegation from the Syrian Community of Terre Haute to meet with him in Indianapolis. During the meeting, they outlined plans for the new church in Terre Haute and immediately began the work of organizing and establishing the parish.

Being a man of action, Fr Antony promised to fulfill his mission regardless of personal hardships and difficulties. From his training at law school, Fr Antony understood the need for clear legal thinking. A constitution was written and notarized on May 6, 1927. It named the community the "St George Syrian Orthodox Society." A board of trustees was organized, and a committee representing the civic community of Terre Haute worked side by side with Fr Antony. A door-to-door drive was initiated at a meeting open to the general public. At this meeting, held in the Central Christian Church, Fr Antony unfolded his plan, gave a comprehensive overview of the fundamental doctrines of the Orthodox Faith, and pointed out the Syrian community's need for a church. Fr Antony stressed the importance of the Church: "Where the Church is, there is the Lord and Savior."

Through Fr Antony's constant efforts and his example to others, the parish took form. With his encouragement, a pledge system was established so as to provide a steady income for the church. Other financial aid came from fundraising efforts such as church socials, dinners, dances, auctions, and raffles. Fr Antony never let an opportunity pass that might bring money into the parish. He continually emphasized the need for the faithful to sacrifice their time and talent, and reminded them of their responsibility to support the church in worship and in work. Many still remember hearing comments such as, "Fr Antony is coming again . . . .I wonder how much money he needs this time? What church is he trying to build? I bet he's collecting for another mission."[2] In 1927, the little immigrant community from Lebanon and Syria saw the realization of its long-cherished dream: the Syrian Orthodox community of Terre Haute had now officially become St George Antiochian Church.

[2]From a conversation with Mr. George Azeze of El Paso, Texas.

Fr. George Rados observes that Fr Antony's ministry in Terre Haute made the Orthodox Church

> ... the center of the social, as well as the religious activities, of the Syrian community. It began to fill the great cultural void that had been unfilled until this time. For its faithful members and for their non-Orthodox friends, this church served as a bridge between the Old World from which they came, and the New World in which they had settled with a deep and sincere desire to become an integral part of the Orthodox Church in this country. Fr Antony set up and taught weekly Arabic classes in conjunction with religious instruction, so that the youth in the community could pray and converse in their mother tongue.[3]

Fr Antony was respected and loved by his people for his sincere devotion and commitment to the service of the Church. He fulfilled his pastorate faithfully, and the parishioners of St George continue to honor his memory. With the church well- established, Fr Antony felt free, in 1930, to accept a new appointment to serve St George Antiochian Church of Detroit.[4]

Detroit, Michigan

In Detroit, Fr Antony spent much of his time writing articles and translating the works of Khalil Gibran. Between his spiritual duties as pastor and his devotion to writing and translating, he had little time to spare. Fr Antony quickly became "a shining star of his time."[5]

He realized early on the importance of using English in the liturgical services. At Terre Haute, he had tried to teach Arabic to the youth. In Detroit, however, he became convinced that made more sense to translate the services from Arabic into English. He collaborated with Fr Seraphim Nassar to bring Professor Habib Kateba from Lebanon in order to translate the *Altazeia-Al-Hakkekeiah* into English. When

[3]George M. Rados, *St. George Orthodox Church.*
[4]Ibid.
[5]From a private interview with Mose Nassar, held in Detroit, Michigan, March 4, 1972.

finished, the trans-lation was called *The Divine Prayers and Services of the Catholic-Orthodox Church of Christ*. Commonly known as the "Nassar book" (and affectionately referred to as the "Five-Pounder"), this translation remains in regular use to this day.

Khalil Gibran

During his missionary days, Fr Antony became a close personal friend of Khalil Gibran. Concerning Antony's Arabic translation of *The Prophet*, a work which Gibran originally composed in English, Gibran said: "Only you could have tailored such a beautiful Arabic garment for my *Prophet*."[6] Although others also translated *The Prophet* into Arabic, Gibran—and most Arabic-speaking readers—clearly favored Antony's translation. Antony also translated other works by Gibran, including *Sand and Foam*, *The Made Man*, *The Forerunner*, *Jesus the Son of Man*, *The Earth of Gods*, and *The Words of Gibran*.

Fr Antony did not limit his attention to Gibran. He also translated other books into Arabic, including titles such as *Why I Am a Christian* by Dr Frank Crane, *Life of Christ* by Giovanni Pappini, *The Simple Life* by Charles Wagner, *The Man Nobody Knows* by Bruce Barton, and *Today and the Future Day* by A. Brisbane.

Author and Editor

Fr Antony even found time to author several books of his own, including *One Year in Mexico* and *Read and Think by the Master Thinker*.[7] He edited the *Immortals (Al-Kalidat)*, an Arabic educational monthly review that was first published in 1927. He also wrote many articles that appeared in the *Majallat Al-Kalemat (The Word Review)*. At the time, *The Word Review* was edited by Bishop Emmanuel Abo-Hatab, who had been consecrated as the bishop of Montreal on September 11, 1927. Today, the magazine appears in English; called simply *The Word*, it is the official publication of the Antiochian Archdiocese of North America.

[6]Salem, *Metropolitan Antony Bashir*, 13.
[7]William G. Kafoure, *S.O.Y.O Digest* 5.1 (March 1955): 6.

The Task of Translating

In his translations, Fr Antony often indicated to the reader that he did not necessarily agree with everything the author had written. Nevertheless, he translated their words in order to enlighten Arabic readers about Western thought. For example, in his introduction to Tolstoy's *Confession and His Philosophy*, Fr Antony wrote:

> And there is another point I would like to make to the literary reader before he reads these books, namely that my translation of such a book does not confine me whatsoever to the author's ideas and opinions. He is free in his belief as I am in mine. Nevertheless, I admire his eternal literary style even though his is far from perfect eloquence as seen in the repetition of many words on the same page and even in the same expression. I say, in spite of all this, his thinking remains his guide and his process of logic, his companion in his writing.[8]

When translating a work into Arabic, he would revise the text three or four times before submitting it for publication. Because Arabic typewriters were unavailable, every translation was written out by hand. Eventually, he lost the use of some of his fingers as a result of his extensive writing: "He even had to hold a pencil in his fist for the last sixteen or seventeen years of his life."[9]

Fr Antony offered the following rationale for his labors as a translator:

> My duty toward the Christian message, which I serve, has obliged me constantly to travel over the continent of the United States, to serve the souls of my brothers from my homeland. They are scattered over the length and breadth of this country. My spiritual duty is missionary endeavor; however, this does not take more than two or three days a week, so this is why I have enough time to read constantly and write wherever I go.

[8]Khalil Gibran, *Tolstoy's Confession and His Philosophy* (Arabic edition), Antony Bashir, tr. (Cairo: Elias' Modern Press, 1932).

[9]Adele Khoury, personal interview.

I am one of those who believe in work and its sacredness. I am not exaggerating when I say that good works come from faith; that is why I must constantly work. I firmly believe that what I have learned (the knowledge I have gained) can be advantageous to others. For this reason I strive never to waste one moment of my time. I write in trains, homes, hotels, and in shopping centers. Everywhere I go, I find a chair or a stone to sit upon, paper and ink stored all the while in my small suitcase without which I cannot be happy.

Yet even though I have a great interest in individual authorship, I still believe in the necessity of translating the works of great writers and composers of the Western world. For I firmly believe that in their intellectual and economic outlook, they are more knowledgeable than we, and the period of [the last] 300 years that permitted this was not granted to us. Thus by translating their thoughts, which are not found in our thinking and outlook, we can come to an understanding of this creative act.

Above all, I believe that man does not reach intellectual maturity before the age of thirty-five; I am not yet thirty-one. Still reading and writing have to be pursued with patience and quietness; therefore, to those of you who seek my personal writing, I beg you to be patient with me as God is patient with us.[10]

By the time he reached his early thirties, Fr Antony's intellectual abilities in translating and writing had made him well known among the Syrian-Lebanese people both in this country and abroad. Even his commission as missionary priest did not impede his literary work. He captured the hearts of many who became fond of his strong personality and character.

His dedication and devotion to the Church and to his people ultimately led him to the highest position in the Antiochian Archdiocese of North America. After serving the Detroit community for five years, Fr Antony was elected as a bishop by the Holy Synod. At the hands of Patriarch Alexander III of Antioch, he was consecrated Archbishop of New York and North America.

[10]Gibran, *Tolstoy's Confession.*

CHAPTER 5

The Election of
Metropolitan Antony

Because of the vacancy in the Archbishopric of New York and all
North America, due to the death of its canonical shepherd of
thrice-blessed memory, the late Victor Abou-Assaley, who died
April 19, 1934, and due to the need of the Archdiocese for a good
shepherd to take care of this flock, we have delegated His Eminence, our beloved brother in Christ, Theodosius, Metropolitan
of Tyre and Sidon, in accordance with our Patriarchal encyclical
dated June 23, 1935, No. 424, to go to New York City, the seat
of the Vacant Archdiocese, to supervise and preside over the
canonical nomination . . .

—Alexander III of Antioch[1]

For almost fourteen months before his consecration, Archimandrite Antony Bashir, pastor of St George Church in Detroit,
acted as the vicar of the patriarch in administering the Syrian
Orthodox Archdiocese. After all the pressure, mistrust, and confusion
that had reigned from 1914 to 1934, the Syrian parishes were forced
to choose a new leader. The pride, jealousy, and relative wealth of the
various factions—whose loyalties remained divided among the
mother church (Antioch), the Russian Church, and the followers of
Metropolitan Germanos—only enhanced the complexity of the task
of electing a bishop to succeed Victor Abou-Assaley.

---

[1]*Patriarchal Manifesto Praxis*, October 25, 1936. Found in the Archives of the
Antiochian Orthodox Christian Archdiocese in Englewood, NJ.

The Candidates

The leaders of the three factions were the Archimandrites Antony Bashir, Samuel David, and Ananias Kassab. Metropolitan Theodosius of Tyre and Sidon, who later became Patriarch of Antioch, traveled to the United States to oversee the election. Prior to his arrival, the three factions exchanged letters and held heated discussions. In spite of the tension that preceded the election, each man vowed to unite the archdiocese and to support the newly elected archbishop on the condition that he was canonically elected by the people.

Upon the arrival of Metropolitan Theodosius, the three participants signed a letter stating the following:

1. They had agreed to devote their lives to the service of the holy Orthodox Church;

2. They had agreed to the Encyclical Letter, dated June 23, 1935, that called for a legal and just election by the majority of the voters;

3. They had agreed to maintain two districts as bishoprics in the archdiocese: one bishopric on the West Coast (the seat being in Los Angeles, California), and one bishopric in the Midwest (with its seat either in Toledo, Ohio, or Detroit, Michigan);

4. And they had agreed that the consecration would take place before the Patriarchal Delegate left again for Damascus.[2]

Upon signing, all participants agreed that personal ambition would play no part in the election. Their sole intention was to do what was best for the Church in North America.

Political Maneuvering

Later history, however, reveals that Archimandrite Samuel David yielded to the temptation to personal ambition. Although Ananias

[2]Letter from Patriarchal Delegate Metropolitan Theodosius dated October 15, 1935. Found in the Archives of the Antiochian Orthodox Christian Archdiocese in Englewood, NJ.

remained faithful to the agreement, he later stated that he considered the election non-canonical. In November 1936, he wrote in *Al-Neser*, an Arabic-language newspaper, that "there is true evidence that the mastermind of the election to the Antiochian archbishopric was Bishop Niphon Saba, who had indicated that Archimandrite Ananias would never have the opportunity to be elected as a bishop in the United States as long as he lived."[3] In the same newspaper, Ananias stated that, prior to the election, Antony had promised him an appointment as personal secretary of the archdiocese, were Antony elected. The mistrust and confusion that existed prior to the election tainted not only the election itself, but eventually led to a break in the archdiocese.

The Election

After lengthy deliberations with all the factions, Metropolitan Theodosius set the election for Sunday, November 10, 1935, in Detroit, Michigan, from 1:00 P.M. to 7:00 P.M. The official list of nominees included Archimandrites Antony Bashir of Douma, Samuel David of Aitha, Agapios Golam of Beirut, and Ananias Kassab. Eventually, the election came down to just Bashir and David.[4] At the time of the election, "Samuel David was serving a parish in Toledo, Ohio. A vote was taken with [Antony] and David as the candidates. Montreal, Boston, and Worcester were split 50/50. The West strongly favored [Antony] as the bishop. [Antony] won the election by a majority."[5]

Within six months of this election, however, the unity of the archdiocese would be shattered. In a letter written to Archimandrite Ananias Kassab and dated March 25, 1936, Archbishop-elect Antony Bashir laid out his proposal for peace:

I would like to inform you that last week I wrote a letter to His Beatitude, our Patriarch, and to the Holy Synod asking them

[3]Letter of Ananias Kassab to Antony Bashir, dated 1936. Found in the Archives of the Antiochian Orthodox Christian Archdiocese in Englewood, NJ.
[4]Ibid., 12.
[5]From a personal interview with Rev. Raphael Husson.

about the diocese and its many spiritual needs. I need a bishop to assist me in the ministry. He would take an honorary title without a diocese or an archdiocese of any specific area and without a vote in the Synod, very much like the arrangement that exists in regard to the vicar of the Archbishop of Beirut. In addition to this request, I ask that his honorary title be "Archbishop of Toledo" and that my new title be "Metropolitan of New York and all North America." This suggestion is acceptable to all parties. Even today His Eminence, the delegate of the patriarch, has sent an article summing up this request to the newspapers. Our dear brother Samuel is with us in Grand Rapids, and he is in good health. He is pleased over the new arrangement.[6]

The Toledo Agreement

At a meeting in Toledo, the patriarchal representative was asked to consecrate Samuel David as an auxiliary to Metropolitan Antony. Antony, moreover, was to assist at the consecration of David. The representative accepted the compromise that Antony would be first hierarch, with David as his assistant. A letter was sent to the patriarch asking his blessing for this undertaking.[7] Theodosius, the patriarchal delegate, wrote a letter to Archimandrite Samuel David in which he explained that he fully intended to consecrate him as assistant to Metropolitan Antony before leaving the country. Here is a translation of the Arabic text of his letter:[8]

> Our beloved son in the Lord, Archimandrite Samuel David,
>   Extending our blessing and prayers, we thank you for your sincere hospitality during our visit with you and your beloved

[6]Found in the Archives of the Antiochian Orthodox Christian Archdiocese in Englewood, NJ. Antony's letter is a reply to a letter from Archimandrite Ananias Kassab. Kassab made the letter available by having it published in the daily *Al-Naser*.

[7]Husson, personal interview.

[8]Letter of Theodosius to Archimandrite Samuel David, dated April 7, 1936. Found in the Archives of the Antiochian Orthodox Christian Archdiocese in Englewood, NJ.

parish. Also we inform you that we have received the telegram that was sent from Toledo today, and also we have received the letters of our spiritual children Mr Burber Farise, Mr Kalil Ashkar, Mr Abdalla Khoury, and Mr Abdalla Kasses. In reply to them, we would like to address you with the sincerity of a loving father for his faithful son, saying: We came to this country motivated by the peace of our beloved people. And for the peace we have worked, and we are still working unceasingly. You know that for the sake of peace we met in Detroit and, being inspired by the wish of his Eminence, the elected Archbishop, we presented our report and that of his Eminence to His Beatitude our Patriarch concerning the request of an assistant to the Archbishop-elect.

We also asked His Beatitude that the title of the Archbishop be Metropolitan and that of the assistant be Archbishop. We sincerely thought the answer would come in less than six weeks. You also know, beloved son, that many objections arose against this arrangement . . . Yet, we assure you that we are continuing to do our best to bring this arrangement to its fulfillment . . . So be confident and reassure our beloved on your side and everywhere regarding the orders of His Beatitude our Patriarch, that the consecration of the Metropolitan should take place first; and immediately he, the Metropolitan-elect, will present a new petition confirming the first petition about the need for an assistant, and we, in our turn, will write our report, trying our best to solve the problem according to God's will. Also we promise you before God that we will not leave this Archdiocese before the consecration of the assistant takes place in the manner that we have already indicated. In respect to the exact date of the consecration we cannot give a decisive word. However, we think that it will very probably be as soon as possible in accordance with the ecclesiastical laws.

Also be sure, beloved son, that we are seeking peace between the people who are around you as well as among the other group and, as you blame us, so they do likewise.

Arm yourself with patience and confidence and do not anticipate things before their due time and the Great Lord will fulfill
your desires as well as ours. Amen.

Theodosius
Patriarchal Delegate
Metropolitan of Tyre and Sidon
and its Dependencies.

Written in Brooklyn, April 7, 1936

Thus both the letter of Metropolitan-elect Antony and the letter of
the patriarchal delegate reveal a willingness on the part of all concerned to bring peace and harmony to the Orthodox faithful of the
Antiochian Archdiocese. In his letter, the patriarchal delegate even
declared that the consecration of an assistant would occur before his
departure. His letter was published in the Arabic-language newspaper
in Brooklyn so that every member of the Archdiocese would be
informed of the patriarchal representative's good intentions. The consecration of Samuel as Metropolitan Antony's assistant was the obvious solution to the growing division. Factions existed, favoritism ran
high, and politics played its role. For this reason, the patriarchal delegate instructed Samuel to "arm himself with patience and confidence,"[9] assuring him that the consecration would take place soon.

Whose Monkey Business Was It?

Over the course of the next nine days, however, things changed. On
April 16, 1936, the patriarchal delegate stopped in Lansing, Michigan, and sent a wire advising the patriarch to ignore the letter sent previously from Toledo. When the representatives who had been at
Toledo heard what had been done, their reaction was that "if the
patriarch wants to play such monkey-business, then we can treat him
in the same way."[10] This reversal of position by the patriarch's delegate (asking the patriarch to delay his decision on the consecration of

[9]Ibid.
[10]Raphael Husson, personal interview.

Samuel David as an assistant) greatly increased the mistrust and lack of confidence already present within the archdiocese.[11]

Fr Samuel David had served for sixteen years as pastor of St George Syrian Orthodox Church in Toledo. Influenced by country-men from his hometown of Aitha, and stung by the apparent betrayal by the patriarchal delegate, Samuel yielded to their calls that he become archbishop without consideration for the canons of the Church.

Time magazine reported the events as follows:

> When Samuel David failed to win the contest, he promptly charged that it had been uncanonically conducted. Archbishop Theodosius offered to compromise by elevating both [Antony] and David, then withdrew that offer. Feeling he had been double-crossed, Samuel David marshaled Syrian followers about him. By last week he was ready to declare himself Syrian Archbishop of North America. Though he could find high Syrian prelates willing to dabble with him in muddied Church water, he lined up three sympathetic Russian bishops whose spiritual powers were, after all, as efficacious as those of any Orthodox Churchmen.[12]

The Russian bishops were Archbishop Adam Phillipovsky of Philadelphia, Bishop Arseny Chuhovits of Detroit, and Bishop Leonty Turkevich of Chicago. All were members of the Russian Orthodox Church. They took upon themselves the responsibility of going ahead with the consecration without consulting the Patriarch of Antioch, the patriarchal delegate, or their own spiritual father, Metropolitan Theophilus.[13]

Two Consecrations

On Sunday, April 19, 1936, Archimandrite Samuel was consecrated bishop and, during the same liturgy, elevated to archbishop. On the

[11]Ibid.

[12]*Time Magazine* (May 4, 1936): 10.

[13]see the letter of Theodosius to Theophilos, dated April 26, 1936. Antiochian Archdiocese Archives.

very same day, at St Nicholas Cathedral in Brooklyn, New York, during the Divine Liturgy celebrated by His Eminence Metropolitan Theodosius of Tyre and Sidon and His Eminence Archbishop Vitaly of the Russian Orthodox Church in North America, "Archimandrite Antony Bashir was consecrated by the grace of the Most-Holy Spirit, canonical Archbishop of the divinely-preserved Archdiocese of New York and all North America."[14]

As was stated in the Patriarchal Manifest (Praxis) of Alexander III, the Patriarch of Antioch:

> It is therefore the duty of all the faithful within the boundaries of his diocese and under his jurisdiction, of the clergy and laity, to offer to him all their obedience, respect, and honor, and to give him due loyalty and love, and to be faithful and obedient to his orders, and to conform to and to abide by his decisions, and to remember his canonical name . . . No one will have any authority to oppose him in anything or to object to his authority or decisions . . . in accordance with the biblical exhortation and holy canons.[15]

A Russian Mess

Informed of the consecration of Samuel David, Metropolitan Theodosius and the newly consecrated Archbishop Antony sent a letter of protest to Metropolitan Theophilus, the head of the Russian Orthodox Church in the United States. In reply, Theophilus wrote:

> Your kind letter of April 25 in regard to the consecration of Samuel has been received and puzzled me very much . . . since I do not have any information about this consecration performed by our bishops. I consider it my duty to inform your Eminence that the decision about the validity of the consecration should be placed in the hands of His Beatitude, the Patriarch of Antioch and the East, Alexander III.[16]

[14]Ibid.
[15]Ibid.
[16]Letter of Theophilus to Theodosius, dated May 4, 1936. Found in the Archives of the Antiochian Orthodox Christian Archdiocese in Englewood, NJ.

The non-canonical behavior of his bishops led Metropolitan Theophilus to present the case to the convention of Russian Orthodox bishops meeting in Pittsburgh. According to the minutes of this convention, dated May 18, 1936, the three afore-mentioned bishops justified themselves, saying that they had the right and power to act by consecrating Samuel. They defended their actions on three grounds.

Firstly, they addressed the negative telegram sent by patriarchal representative Theodosius to the Patriarch of Antioch, in which he asked for a delay in the consecration of Samuel. They noted that this telegram had produced an extreme reaction among Samuel's supporters and had caused them to seek other means to secure his consecration. Secondly, the supporters of Samuel had repeatedly warned that they would leave the Orthodox Church if the consecration did not take place. And lastly, the bishops stated that the Russian Orthodox Church had historically looked after the ecclesiastical and jurisdictional matters of the Syrian Church from its inception in North America. They pointed out that the Russian Church had previously consecrated bishops such as Raphael, Aftimios, Emmanuel, and Sofronios.[17]

These three reasons, however, failed to convince the majority of the bishops of the validity of the consecration. "A vote was taken, in which the results were three to five, the majority being in favor of not recognizing the consecration."[18] Archbishop Tikhon, who was one of the five rejecting the consecration, emphasized the invalidity of the consecration and pleaded with the bishops present to continue the brotherly relationship between the Antiochian and the Russian churches.

An Appeal to the Russian Synod

In order to avoid divisions with the Russian Church, the five bishops who opposed the consecration declared that the case should be pre-

[17]See the Letter of Archbishop Adam to Metropolitan Theodosius, dated April 22, 1936. Found in the Archives of the Antiochian Orthodox Christian Archdiocese in Englewood, NJ.

[18]Ibid.

sented to the Russian Synod of Bishops at Sremsky Karlovtsy, Yugoslavia, "in that this synod has the supreme authority and jurisdiction over all the Russian clergy outside Russia."[19] On January 31, 1938, an excommunication entitled *General Manifesto* was jointly declared by the Synod of Bishops at Sremsky Karlovtsy and by the Patriarch of Antioch, Alexander III. The text of this decision read:

> Whereas, Archimandrite Samuel David is a clergyman under the jurisdiction of the Patriarch of Antioch, and was one of the candidates for the Episcopate of the Church of Antioch, whose names were submitted to the patriarch for election and approval;
>
> And whereas, his consecration as Bishop was performed by Archbishop Adam, Bishop Arseni, and Bishop Leonty, without canonical election, and without the approval of the Patriarch of Antioch nor under the approval of the Russian Ecclesiastical Authority;
>
> And whereas, this consecration was contrary to the following Canons: No. 35 of the Canons of the Holy Apostles, No. 4 of the First Ecumenical Council, No. 2 of the Second Ecumenical Council, Nos. 13, 9, and 22 of the Council of Antioch, No. 15 of the Council of Sardinis, and No. 15 of the Council of Carthage, therefore, we declare the said consecration to be non-canonical;
>
> And whereas, Archimandrite Samuel David is a clergyman under the jurisdiction of the Church of Antioch, therefore the decision as to his responsibility for accepting such consecration and decision on his future canonical status is hereby left to the judgment of the Church of Antioch.
>
> Therefore, we hereby declare to all our spiritual children, clergy, and laity, in all parts of the Archdiocese of New York and North America, that Archimandrite Samuel David, being disobedient to the Higher Ecclesiastical Authority and to the local authority of the Archdiocese of New York and all North America, and having stolen the Grace of God through worldly means, and assuming to himself the office of the Episcopate, is hereby declared

---

[19]Letter of Theophilos to Theodosius, dated May, 4, 1936. Antiochian Archdiocese Archives.

excommunicated from the ecclesiastical Communion, and we forbid the clergy and the laity to have communion with him . . .[20]

Attached to the above *General Manifesto* was a letter from Archbishop Antony Bashir that read, "It is also submitted for official information to all religious bodies, government offices in America, and all public newspapers for publication to protect the innocent citizens from falling into the misrepresentation and deceit of this excommunicated clergyman who has no ecclesiastical permission to perform any religious ministration of any kind."[21]

[20]*General Manifesto*, dated January 31, 1938. Found in the Archives of the Antiochian Orthodox Christian Archdiocese in Englewood, NJ.

[21]Found in the Archives of the Antiochian Orthodox Christian Archdiocese in Englewood, NJ.

CHAPTER 6

Efforts at Reconciliation

Almost two years elapsed before the aforementioned edict of excommunication was declared. During these two years, attempts were made on both sides to bring this chaotic episode to an end. Meetings of faithful clergy and laity were held immediately after the consecration. Archimandrite Ananias Kassab, foremost among the supporters of Samuel David and well known among his fellow clergy, played an important role in securing a peaceful agreement. Ananias publicly declared in the Arabic-language newspaper *El-Nasir*, "The desire to solve this endless division can be accomplished only on one condition, that Samuel write a letter of apology to the patriarch asking forgiveness for his non-canonical consecration and, further, that he indicate his intentions to be obedient to and to assist the newly elected Archbishop of New York and all North America, Metropolitan Antony Bashir."[1] Ananias' proposal gained wide support and was endorsed by both the clergy and the laity of the archdiocese.

Letter of Apology

In a first step toward implementing this proposal, Archimandrite Ananias summoned Samuel David from Charleston, West Virginia, to Montreal, Canada, on December 17, 1936, to write a letter of apology. Extensive discussions took place between Samuel and his followers at the home of Alexander Shati'la in Montreal. On the same day,

---

[1]Letter of Ananias Kassab published in *El-Nasir* Newspaper. Found in the Archives of the Antiochian Orthodox Christian Archdiocese in Englewood, NJ.

December 17, Samuel signed the letter and departed for his residence in Charleston in the hopes that this letter would bring harmony to the archdiocese.

On the following day, December 18, the letter of apology was submitted to the patriarchal delegate, Metropolitan Theodosius, and to the newly elected Archbishop Antony for their approval. Since the letter failed to clarify the nature of Samuel's service in the United States, it was rejected. In actuality, the metropolitan wanted Samuel to declare that he had no desire to serve in the Archdiocese of New York, but rather wished to be transferred to another archdiocese in South America. According to Archimandrite Kassab, this request was not even mentioned in his previous consultation with Metropolitan Theodosius.

An Uneasy Peace

An uneasy peace settled on the archdiocese. In view of past history, Samuel David and Antony Bashir both wanted to adhere to the canons of the Church and avoid any further ordinations of those who were seeking holy orders through improper means or with the help of rebellious individuals. At the parish level, however, confusion with regard to the rejection of Samuel's letter of apology spread among the clergy and laity. The letter's rejection by the patriarchal delegate gave credence to those who claimed that the election of Archbishop Antony had been fixed. The rejection of the letter disappointed others who had waited in vain for Metropolitan Theodosius to fulfill his promise to assist in Samuel's consecration.

A Slide Toward Division

As 1938 drew to a close, the division within the archdiocese began to manifest itself. Archbishop Antony, with his charismatic leadership, undertook his archpastoral responsibilities in full obedience to the mother church. Bishop Samuel carried out his duties in the few churches that supported him in spite of his excommunication. Other clergy and parishes remained neutral, declaring loyalty to the Patriarch of Antioch instead.

During this unfortunate period, Archbishop Antony manifested his intention to obey the canons. He was a determined man of convictions who never allowed himself to neglect Church matters. He feared neither expressing the truth nor acting upon it. He simply sought the good of the archdiocese. As reported in the *The Syrian Eagle*, Archbishop Antony excommunicated five clergy who deliberately encouraged Bishop Samuel: Archimandrite Ananias Kassab, Archimandrite Basilios Nader, Fr Michael Zarbatani, Fr Michael El-Nekit, and Fr Raphael Husson.

Along with disciplining the clergy as needed, Antony also cared for his flock, traveling from one city to another, establishing mission churches and providing them with educated clergy. He alone was responsible for the administration of the archdiocese. "He had the sole jurisdiction over everything; the laity had nothing to do with anything in regard to the life of the Church, financially or otherwise."[2]

High Hopes

In March 1939, the Patriarch of Antioch sent a letter rehabilitating Bishop Samuel and accepted him back into the Church. As a result, Bishop Samuel was given the title of archbishop while Archbishop Antony was granted the title of metropolitan. Thus, Metropolitan Antony remained head of the Archdiocese of New York and all North America, as declared in the Praxis of 1936, and Archbishop Samuel was made the bishop of Toledo within Metropolitan Antony's jurisdiction. The Holy Synod agreed to these arrangements with the expectation that harmony and peace would thereby prevail.

Reorganizing the Archdiocese

Metropolitan Antony was advised to call an Archdiocesan convention, and he agreed to a gathering in Brooklyn, New York, on September 24–28, 1947. At the convention, a plan for reorganizing the

---

[2]From a personal interview with Mr Monsour H. Laham, July 15, 1972, in Boston, MA.

archdiocese was introduced. It was decided that the constitution and by-laws of the archdiocese should remain as they were until the next convention, which was to be held in 1948 in Detroit, Michigan.

At the 1947 Convention, it was decided unanimously to adopt a proposal known as "The Plan" for the complete reorganization of the Archdiocese. Proposed by the delegates from the churches of St George and St John Damascene in Boston, and by Messrs Monsour H. Laham, John C. Khouri, and Fozi Cahaly, "The Plan" was

> a sensational setup that took the delegates like wild fire. But the test was . . . the vote at the General Assembly . . . .The followers of [Bishop] Samuel and Archimandrite Kassab, who, I believe, was vicar at the time, were quite unhappy with it and did not particularly care to support it. They tried to do all that they could to have the plan fail. Before the General Assembly, I personally went up to visit [Bishop] Samuel's room to meet with him in the presence of his vicar, Kassab. I pleaded with both of them to support the plan for the best interest of the Church. In the plan there had been provided a position for Auxiliary Bishops.[3]

The next year, in 1948, a national convention was held in Detroit for purpose of ratifying the constitution that had been written previously, and for re-evaluating all aspects of church administration. Of this meeting, Mr Monsour Laham recalls the following:

> Our brothers of the other group were unhappy and did not join us. We even had members of their group on our board, but . . . we did not receive any financial support from them. But they met with us and were part of us for awhile . . . They did not seem free to go along with it . . . When I said to Bishop Samuel and Ananias that we were going to be as we had been before our troubles in earlier years . . . Ananias Kassab said to me, "You are trying to make us part of you. When were we ever part of you to join with you now?"[4]

[3]Ibid.
[4]Ibid.

Unfortunately, this situation continued until 1953, when Bishop Samuel met again with the convention in Detroit. During the five years that had passed since the 1948 Convention, Metropolitan Antony continued to seek peace. "All this time Antony was wanting to reach an agreement with him, and a number of times did so."[5] For example, Metropolitan Antony declared in his report (included in the *Transactions of the Sixth Convention of the Archdiocese* in 1951, over which he presided and at which Archbishop Samuel David served as vice-chairman) that

> . . . our Archdiocese today, thanks to Almighty God, enjoys peace and harmony through the cooperation and Christian devotion and loyalty of the churches and parishes, plus the sincere efforts of His Eminence, Archbishop Samuel David of Toledo. We have been working most harmoniously in attending to the spiritual needs of our parishioners in America.[6]

A Question of Succession

In 1953, according to Fr Paul Schneirla, an agreement was reached whereby if one bishop died, whichever bishop survived would be recognized as the Metropolitan of New York and all North America. Every parish in North America would then be subject to his jurisdiction. However, he notes that

> . . . none of these agreements were kept by the Toledo group. Perhaps it is because they claim that we [referring to the New York Archdiocese] violated the agreements, but I am sure that we did not. However, Antony's idea was to reach an agreement whereby they would exist together with Samuel as his subordinate, but if this failed, to absorb their parishes and clergy one by one or any other way.[7]

Metropolitan Antony was not the only one who hoped to end this division; the laity also shared this hope. At the Archdiocesan Conven-

[5]From a personal interview with Rev. Paul Schneirla.
[6]Report of Metropolitan Antony, *Transactions of the Sixth Convention*, 1951.
[7]Schneirla, personal interview.

tion of 1953 in Detroit, an official proposal was set forth regarding the successor to Metropolitan Antony. Mr Monsour Laham recalled:

> We made a proposition to our brother of what by then had begun to be known as the Toledo group . . . Because of the unfortunate developments which widened the rift, we came up with a suggestion: The proposition that if Archbishop Antony died before Archbishop Samuel, that Arch-bishop Samuel David would automatically succeed to the head of the Archdiocese pending the approval of the patriarch. However, if Arch-bishop David died, there would be no more Toledo followers. But it all referred to one group. That was our plan.[8]

An entire day was devoted to the discussion of how to safeguard the unity of the Archdiocese and how best to protect against divisions in the future. To this end, the Convention unanimously accepted the following decisions.[9]

> Whereas: In order to protect the unity and peace of the Syrian Antiochian Orthodox Archdiocese of New York and all North America, and to insure the continuation of that unity;
>
> And Whereas: To create and establish a definite and certain procedure for the nomination and election of a qualified successor to the present Metropolitan Archbishop in the event of his decease or resignation;
>
> BE IT THEREFORE RESOLVED:
>
> 1. That upon the death or resignation of the present Metropolitan Bashir, His Grace Archbishop Samuel David shall automatically succeed to the office of Metropolitan Archbishop of the Syrian Antiochian Orthodox Archdiocese of New York and all North America; and
>
> 2. Immediately upon the decease of Archbishop Samuel David, or in the event of succession to the office of Metropolitan Archbishop, the existence of the present Archdiocese of Toledo and

---

[8]Monsour Laham, personal interview.
[9]*S.O.Y.O Digest*, 5. 4 (December 1955).

Dependencies shall automatically be terminated, and no successor to Archbishop Samuel shall be elected; and

3. In the event of the decease or resignation of both the metropolitan and the archbishop, the new metropolitan archbishop of the Archdiocese of New York and all North America shall be chosen in the following manner:

A. Within sixty days the secretary of the Archdiocese Board of Trustees shall, by written notice, call a special meeting of all the clerical and lay delegates of all the parishes of the Archdiocese, together with the members of the Archdiocese Board of Trustees, and

B. At this special meeting qualified candidates for the office of metropolitan archbishop shall be chosen by secret ballot of the clerical and lay delegates present, or by an accredited written proxy; from such candidates so chosen, the three who receive the highest number of votes shall be considered properly nominated, and their names shall be submitted to His Beatitude, the Patriarch of Antioch and the Holy Synod, for the election of the three nominated candidates as metropolitan archbishop of the Syrian Antiochian Archdiocese of New York and all North America.[10]

This proposal however, did not meet with the approval of all the delegates. Mr Laham noted the lack of accord:

I think our brothers thought we were pulling a "fast one" on them. God knows who would outlive whom. Though all in their group did not favor the plan, neither did all in our group favor it. However, I must say to you, that our group finally reached an agreement and accepted the proposal . . . But our brothers were skeptical. They did not agree to it. But it did temper the rift from then until 1955.[11]

[10]Ibid.
[11]Monsour Laham, personal interview.

A Rose by Any Other Name: A Question of Titles

As previously discussed, Bishop Samuel had been "rehabilitated" by the Patriarch of Antioch in March 1939. Upon his rehabilitation, Bishop Samuel received the title of archbishop while, at the same time, Archbishop Antony was elevated to the rank of metropolitan. These titles enabled both hierarchs to better define their high offices.

In the fall of 1955, Archbishop Samuel went to Syria to attend the celebration of the fiftieth anniversary of the Patriarch, His Beatitude Alexander III. While Samuel was in Syria, Patriarch Alexander elevated him to the rank of metropolitan. This action by the patriarch naturally created a furor among the faithful of the Archdiocese. Samuel's elevation to this rank was advertised in the papers, and telegrams were sent to his supporters prior to his return to the United States.

The patriarch explained his actions in an interview with the members of the Lebanese Press, in which he said that "the condition of the Archdiocese of Toledo, Ohio, was discussed in this meeting [of the Synod], and it was decided to raise the status of Archbishop Samuel of the Syrian Orthodox Archdiocese of Toledo, Ohio, to the rank of metropolitan."[12] However, Bishop Elia Saliba, after investigating the status of Archbishop Samuel as "metropolitan," found that he "had received a letter from Patriarch [Alexander] Tahan elevating him to the rank of metropolitan." Bishop Elia emphasized that this was "solely the action of the patriarch himself."[13] The elevation of Samuel to metropolitan was apparently never a decision of the Holy Synod, nor do any records exist in the Holy Synod of Archbishop Samuel's "elevation."[14]

One Archdiocese or Two?

It remains a mystery as to why Patriarch Alexander gave Samuel this new title. It was immediately clear, however, that Metropolitan

[12]William G. Kafoure, *S.O.Y.O. Digest* 5. 4. (December 1955): 5.

[13]From a personal interview with Elia Saliba, held September 20, 1972, in Englewood, NJ.

[14]Ibid.

Samuel and his supporters were trying to divide the archdiocese into two independent entities. It had always been the position of the Archdiocese of New York that there had only ever been one archdiocese in North America, in accordance with the original Praxis. However, the patriarch's statement to the Lebanese press at the time—namely, that "it was decided to raise the status of Archbishop Samuel of the Syrian Orthodox Archdiocese of Toledo, Ohio, to the rank of metropolitan"[15]—indicates that there were those, including the patriarch, who considered Toledo a separate archdiocese, and not merely a diocese within the Archdiocese of New York.

One cannot deny the existence of the Toledo group. However, neither Metropolitan Antony nor the members of his flock regarded them as a separate archdiocese. In the first place, the Toledo churches had never seceded from the Syrian Antiochian Archdiocese itself. While the Toledo group often behaved as if it were separate and independent, there was never any formal statement of separation. Furthermore, Metropolitan Antony always maintained his strong opposition to a creation of two separate archdioceses.

Upon Metropolitan Samuel's return to the United States, the situation calmed. In December of 1955, both metropolitans were invited to a celebration in Boston. At this time, Metropolitan Samuel laid out his plan, which revealed his aspirations for elevation to the rank of metropolitan. This plan became the basis for later misunderstandings about his status. Monsour Laham, who was involved with the Toledo problem from the beginning, explained how this came about: "While I was with Metropolitan Antony in his suite, I received a phone call from Miss Mary Douad. She proposed a private conversation concerning the status and relationship of the two hierarchs."[16] Finally, a meeting was held in the presence of Archbishop Samuel, Mary Douad, and her sister Anna, and for the last time a direct conversation took place between Monsour Laham and Archbishop Samuel regarding the Toledo Diocese and its archbishop.

Monsour Laham asked Samuel, "Do you believe in this division?" The archbishop replied, "No, I do not believe in division and have

[15]Kafoure, *S.O.Y.O. Digest* 5. 4. (December 1955): 5.
[16]Monsour Laham, personal interview.

never wanted a division. All I want is to take care of the churches that follow me." Laham replied, "I don't see any difference in our positions. If that is all you want, we have never denied it to you. You have always been part of us; you are taking care of your people. We have no objection to that; we only differ as to whether you are a separate archdiocese." The archbishop said, "I had no intention of separating." Then Samuel wrote in Arabic what he wanted, namely: *one archdiocese with Samuel having the pastoral care of the churches that had been under his jurisdiction for many years.*[17]

Waiting for Muddy Waters to Clear

The existence of two metropolitans certainly created the appearance of two independent archdioceses. In order to prevent appearances from becoming reality, Metropolitan Antony, in a letter dated April 16, 1956, sought clarification from Antioch "regarding the unity of the Archdiocese of New York and all North America, and its relations with Archbishop Samuel."[18]

Patriarch Alexander replied in a letter dated May, 11, 1956:

In our last letters to Your Eminence, we have repeatedly addressed you as Metropolitan of New York and all North America, and have assured you that rumors about the division of the Archdiocese were without our knowledge. And we promised you in writing that those false rumors will be corrected officially in the first meeting of the General Council—in spite of the fact that this matter is completely under the jurisdiction of the Holy Synod—and all this confusion has happened only because the decisions of the Holy Synod during the old and new meetings were not studied carefully. Therefore we ask you to wait for our final answer on this subject in the meeting of the Holy Synod about the middle of this month, and then we will make the Holy Synod decide finally in this matter in a way that will be most pleasing to Your Eminence.

[17]Ibid.
[18]*The Word* 1. 2 (February 1957): 51.

The next three months turned into an anxious period of waiting for the promised decision by the Holy Synod. Finally, on August 4, 1956, Metropolitan Antony received the following cablegram from Patriarch Alexander:

> Antiochian Holy Synod recognizes only one Archdiocese in North America by the name of New York and all North America—Letter follows.

Rejoicing in the Good News

Delighted by the good news from Antioch, Metropolitan Antony and the board "decided to cable our thanks immediately to His Beatitude and the Holy Synod and to regard the whole matter finally explained: that there is only ONE UNDIVIDED ARCHDIOCESE IN NORTH AMERICA."[19] They sent the following cable to the patriarch and the Holy Synod of Antioch:

> In the name of all the clergy and people of the Archdiocese, we thank Your Beatitude and the Holy Synod for your most wise cable which restored peace to our archdiocese. Your letter is anxiously awaited. God grant you many years of health and happiness.[20]

The archdiocesan board unanimously desired to contact Metropolitan Samuel with what—to them—was good news. A telephone call was made, but Metropolitan Samuel could not be reached; he was en route from Texas, where he had been visiting, and would not arrive in Toledo until the next day. Board members spoke with Archimandrite Ananias Kassab, who answered in the absence of His Eminence. He was asked to relay the message to Metropolitan Samuel. They also stressed, in their conversation with Kassab, their sincere wish to have both Metropolitan Antony and Metropolitan Samuel attend the forthcoming Archdiocese convention.[21]

[19]Ibid.
[20]Ibid.
[21]Ibid.

Peaceful Unity at Last?

Both sides agreed to the unity of the archdiocese. In the presence of Metropolitan Antony and Archbishop Samuel, reconciliation was once again achieved. An agreement, ratified by both, confirmed the unity of the Archdiocese of North America for all time. This agreement was signed on December 13, 1956, in Boston, Massachusetts, in the presence of Monsour Laham, Mary Douad, and Anna Douad, who attended the meeting with the two archbishops.

One United Church in North America

The good news of a united church was sent out to all the parishes. The agreement, entitled *One United Church in North America,* was printed and sent to the churches to be read from their pulpits.[22]

IN THE NAME OF THE FATHER AND THE SON AND THE HOLY SPIRIT.

To all our beloved spiritual children in all North America,

We extend our blessings and best wishes for a peaceful New Year, filled with the grace of peace, unity, and love. We are happy to announce that in order to maintain the unity and welfare of our Holy Church in North America and to clear the misunderstandings arising from recent happenings and events, we declare with full sincerity that, we, Antony, Metropolitan of New York and all North America, and Samuel, Metropolitan of Toledo, Ohio and Dependencies, confirm and support the unity of our Holy Church in North America, with each of us continuing in the same duties of administrating in the same manner the churches that have been under his pastoral care for the last twenty years.

In order that this knowledge may come to all who are concerned, and that peace and unity shall prevail in all the churches of North America, a copy of this statement is to be mailed to His Beatitude and the Holy Synod and to every church in the Archdiocese.

[22]Paul Schneirla, *The Word* 1.1 (January 1957): 27.

Signed this thirtieth day of December, nineteen hundred and fifty-six.

METROPOLITAN ANTONY BASHIR
METROPOLITAN SAMUEL DAVID

Trouble Below the Surface

The years 1957 and 1958 gave the outward appearance of peace and harmony within the archdiocese. Unity seemed apparent on many occasions. For example, at the Midwest Region SOYO (Syrian Orthodox Youth Organization) Convention, held in Grand Rapids, Michigan, on July 6, 1957, the two hierarchs celebrated the hierarchal Divine Liturgy together.

However, underneath the surface of these peaceful waters lurked forces bent on division. False rumors continued to spread that North America had two archdioceses instead of one. This rumor was officially reported to His Beatitude, Patriarch Alexander, on May 16, 1958, and he was asked for a final declaration on this issue.

On May 31, 1958, Patriarch Alexander proclaimed:

> With regard to the Archdiocese of New York and all North America, again and again we assure you, as we did in all our past official letters, that in accordance with the decision of the Holy Synod, THERE IS ONLY ONE ARCHDIOCESE IN NORTH AMERICA UNDER THE CANONICAL JURISDICTION OF THE PATRIARCHATE OF ANTIOCH. We will again write the same to His Grace Archbishop Samuel.[23]

A Time of Last Straws

Less than a month later, on June 26, 1958, Metropolitan Antony found it necessary to write a letter addressed to every church and every parish priest under the pastoral care of Archbishop Samuel. This letter was also made public to all the clergy and churches of the archdiocese.

[23]*The Word* 2. 8 (August 1958): 20.

After careful reading of this communication you will understand that we have always regarded these parishes and their priests as a part undivided of the Archdiocese of New York and all North America. Unfortunately, Archbishop Samuel, contrary to the many sacrifices of the Church to keep him united with the Archdiocese, is still insisting and actually dividing the Archdiocese to create an independent schism for himself against the Holy Canons and the orders of the Holy Synod and the patriarch. Therefore, after twenty-two years of patience and love, we find ourselves moved by sacred duties to our office as the shepherd of this Archdiocese, to declare our final decision as follows:

If His Eminence and his group chooses to remain united with our Archdiocese, our hearts and our churches will always be open to them. On the contrary, if they persist in their present policy of division and confusion, we must regard them as persons separated from our Archdiocese and having no communion with us. Effective today, and until further written notice, please do not participate in any ecclesiastical meeting or any religious service with Archbishop David, and do not accept him in your churches until he returns to unity with our Archdiocese.[24]

A Battle Joined and Interrupted

Once the Holy Synod of Antioch had clearly and finally decreed that there was only one archdiocese in North America, it became necessary to manifest that decree in the actual state of affairs. The archdiocese held its breath, waiting to see whether the parishes of the diocese of Toledo would once and for all acknowledge their full membership in the Archdiocese of New York and all North America, or whether, by continuing to follow Archbishop Samuel, they would separate from the archdiocese altogether. Metropolitan Antony's letter was self-explanatory; it did not, by any means, affirm a split with Archbishop Samuel or with the Toledo Diocese. Rather, the letter made it clear that if the Toledo group believed itself to be separated from the arch-

[24]Ibid., 21.

diocese, or if, in fact, they chose to separate from it, it would be by their own initiative.

Six weeks later, on August 12, 1958, and with everything still in the balance, Archbishop Samuel David died suddenly. His death was a shock to Metropolitan Antony, then en route to the general convention of the archdiocese that was to meet in Los Angeles. The sad news of Archbishop Samuel's death aroused great concern among the clergy and the laity of the archdiocese.

Much to his regret, Metropolitan Antony was unable to attend Archbishop Samuel's funeral. He later noted that, owing "to circumstances beyond our control, we were unable to fulfill our brotherly duty by announcing the great loss of our beloved brother in Christ and by participating in his funeral, but we offered prayers daily for the repose of his soul."[25] Archbishop Michael Shaheen, who at this time was still a priest, asserted that Metropolitan Antony was prevented from attending the funeral because the people of Toledo refused to allow him to come. In their opinion, according to Shaheen, Bashir "had broken relations with Toledo a short time prior to the death of David. For a week or so before Archbishop David's death, Metropolitan Antony, speaking at St Elias Church in Toledo, Ohio, had made the comment: "We no longer have anything to do with St George [the cathedral of the Toledo Diocese]."[26]

Antony's remarks were taken by the Toledo group as an indication that he had excommunicated Archbishop Samuel. The resulting hostility towards Antony was so great that those close to him feared he might be assassinated should he attempt to attend the funeral.[27] The Toledo group asked the Patriarchate of Antioch to send a representative in place of Metropolitan Antony. The Patriarchate responded by sending three bishops to the funeral.[28]

On August 26, 1958, Metropolitan Antony was extremely delighted and honored to meet the Metropolitans Ignatius of Hama

[25]*The Word* 2.10 (October 1958): 24.

[26]From a personal interview with Archbishop Michael Shaheen, held in Oklahoma City, OK, 1989.

[27]Ibid.

[28]Raphael Husson, personal interview.

and Athanasius of Basra-Houran, as well as the other representatives of the Patriarchate, who had come to celebrate the ninth day memorial service for Archbishop Samuel's repose. These representatives expressed their wish that all the Orthodox people in North America would continue in zeal, and would labor for the cooperation, unity, and spiritual progress of the Church by removing all the obstacles that might hinder its spiritual mission of love, peace, and unity. Metropolitan Antony designated September 21, 1958, as a day of prayer and memorial services throughout the archdiocese for the repose of Samuel's soul.

Now the achievement of unity lay wholly within the hands of Metropolitan Antony Bashir. The diocese of Toledo passed directly under his leadership, a leadership that was legally and canonically accepted. But, unfortunately, a new struggle had just begun.

CHAPTER 7

Antony Bashir and the Toledo Archdiocese

It is with regret that I must speak again of a shameful condition which still plagues our Archdiocese: The uncertainty about the unity of our beloved Archdiocese. I do not need to review the long history of misunderstanding. You have my letters on the subject, and those of you who have been delegates to past Conventions have personally witnessed some of the stages in this program of personal ambition and sabotage of unity and cooperation.

I want unity and harmony in the work of our Syrian Antiochian Archdiocese, but I am too busy to waste much time on petty quarrels. We want all our people to share the work with us, and build up one strong unified organization which will be a credit to all Syrian-American Orthodox. No one can deny that I have done my utmost through the years to serve unity. Our hearts are open to all. If, on the other hand, some persons take satisfaction in division, which brings the ridicule of outsiders on our Syrian Orthodox people, let the responsibility rest with them.[1]

Metropolitan Anthony Bashir

A Frustrating Loss of Opportunity

The struggle for one, strong, unified archdiocese did not end with the sudden death of Archbishop Samuel David. Although the Toledo diocese should have fallen under Metropolitan Antony's spiritual guid-

[1]Antony Bashir, *The Word* 2. 11 (November 1958): 15.

ance, in practice it did not. Whether the Toledo leadership would have upheld the principles of unity and succession became a moot question following Metropolitan Antony's comments at St Elias Church, words that many interpreted as an excommunication of the Toledo group. As a result of these comments, the Toledo leadership continued to resent Antony and reject his pastoral care, requesting instead from the Holy Synod an opportunity to have their own archbishop heading an independent archdiocese. While a response to the request of Toledo was being sought, the Toledo diocese was administered by its vicar-general, Fr Michael Howard, who later died in an accident.

The Holy Synod's Dilemma: What to Do with Toledo?

The question of what to do with Toledo was once more in the hands of the Holy Synod of Antioch. The Synod made its position quite clear during its General Synod, held at the Patriarchate of Antioch in November, 1958:

> All the minutes of the meetings of the Holy Synod were carefully checked, and nothing was discovered to prove the canonical existence of another archdiocese in North America. About 4 P.M., the Council decided that in North America there is ONLY ONE archdiocese known as the Arch-diocese of New York and all North America under the jurisdiction of the Patriarchate of Antioch. The parishes of Toledo, Ohio and Dependencies were always a part undivided from this Archdiocese. The Council further approved the plan to establish a bishopric under the Archdiocese of New York and all North America, in the name of Toledo, Ohio and Dependencies, with the understanding that this bishopric will have geographic boundaries, and its bishop will be under the jurisdiction of the Metropolitan, commemorating his name in all Divine Services, and this must be done with the full knowledge and approval of the Metropolitan.[2]

---

[2]*The Word* 3. 9 (November 1959): 17.

The Toledo group sharply criticized the Synod's decision and continued to proclaim itself an independent archdiocese. The patriarch convened a General Synod on May 29, 1959, and issued a final decision, which was transmitted to Metropolitan Antony and the faithful in North America:

1. A number of bishoprics should be established in the Archdiocese of New York and all North America, the boundaries of which are to be decided geographically in accordance with the number of people in each bishopric, and with due consideration to the national and regional status of each;

2. To begin with, a bishopric by the name of Toledo and Dependencies is to be established with geographic boundaries decided by the Metropolitan of New York and all North America and the boards of trustees of the parishes in the district;

3. The boundaries of this bishopric shall be approved by the Patriarchal General Council;

4. The bishops of the bishoprics are nominated and elected by the Holy Synod, in accordance with the canons;

5. The bishops shall commemorate the name of the Patriarch and the name of the Metropolitan of the Archdiocese in all their services;

6. The boards of trustees of the bishoprics shall be represented in the Archdiocese Board of Trustees;

7. The Archdiocese of New York and all North America shall have the right to send five delegates to the General Council of the Patriarchate;

8. The other bishoprics shall be established gradually with the approval of the Archdiocese Board of Trustees and the General Council of the Patriarchate.

The above is a correct copy of the minutes.

Signed and sealed,

Executive Secretary of the General Council of the Patriarchate, Abraham Doumani

Damascus, June 4, 1959[3]

North American Efforts at Implementing Unity

Metropolitan Antony and the members of the Archdiocese Board of Trustees met in Detroit, Michigan, on June 27, 1959. The entire morning session was devoted to a careful study of the above documents, and of the ways and means to implement the synodal decision. With the full approval and blessing of Metropolitan Antony, the board decided unanimously:

1) To immediately accept the decision in principle with regard to the unity of the Archdiocese, and to send a copy to all the parishes of the late Metropolitan Samuel inviting them to complete unity with the Archdiocese;

2) Immediately after the complete unity of all the churches in the Archdiocese, the geographic boundaries for a bishopric of Toledo, Ohio and Dependencies, will be established with the full approval of its churches and clergy;

3) In accordance with the canons of the Patriarchate and our Archdiocese, three qualified clergymen will be nominated by the bishopric, and the names of the winning candidates will be submitted to the Holy Synod for the election of the new bishop;

4) A copy of this decision is to be mailed immediately to His Beatitude in Damascus.

---

[3]*The Word* 3. 7 (September 1959): 23. The information cited was 'Voted at the first session of the first meeting of the year 1959, held on Friday morning, May 29, 1959, at the Patriarchal Palace in Damascus. The actions decided on May 29 were then sent to Metropolitan Bashir along with a cover letter dated June 4, 1959. Both the decision and the cover letter were included in the 'Complete, Official Acts of the 1959 Archdiocesan Convention' printed in *The Word* 3. 9 (November 1959).

Nominating a Bishop for Toledo

On January 13, 1960, a special convention was held in Toledo, Ohio, to further examine the unity of the archdiocese and the creation of the new episcopate. Forty-seven churches, with a total of 48,000 members, were represented. Only seven churches, with a total of 2,200 members, were not present. The convention took steps to implement the decision of the Patriarchal General Council of May 29, 1959. Metropolitan Antony submitted the names of nominees for a secret ballot to elect a future auxiliary bishop for the Toledo diocese. Those named included:

Aboud, Archimandrite Gregory—Toronto, Canada
Ghannam, Archimandrite George—Cedar Rapids, Iowa
Kassab, Archimandrite Ananias—Brooklyn, New York
Kazan, Archimandrite Basil—Toledo, Ohio
Khouri, Archimandrite Ellis—Grand Rapids, Michigan
Kurban, Archimandrite Ilyas—Boston, Massachusetts
Saliba, Archimandrite Athanasius—Worcester, Massachusetts
Saliba, Fr Philip—Cleveland, Ohio
Samna, Archimandrite Gabriel—Canton, Ohio
Shaheen, Archimandrite Michael—Montreal, Canada

When Archimandrites Ellis Khouri, George Ghannam, and Gabriel Samne and Fr Philip Saliba declined the nomination, their names were removed from the list. The voting by secret ballot took place immediately. A special committee, comprised of Fr Thomas Ruffin (Detroit), Fr Paul Romley (Pittsburgh), Monsour Laham, and Moussa Souaid, was appointed to make an accurate count of the ballots. The final results were:

94 votes for Archimandrite Ilyas Kurban
81 votes for Archimandrite Ananias Kassab
65 votes for Archimandrite Gregory Aboud
42 votes for Archimandrite Basil Kazan
33 votes for Archimandrite Athanasius Saliba
32 votes for Archimandrite Michael Shaheen

The three with the highest number of votes were officially accepted as candidates. Metropolitan Antony was asked to submit the names to the patriarch, in order that the Holy Synod of Antioch might elect one of them as bishop of Toledo and assistant to the metropolitan of the archdiocese.[4]

Strange Silence in Antioch

Antony submitted the names promptly to the patriarch and Holy Synod immediately following the Special Convention in Toledo. When no reply was received from the patriarch,

> we wrote again repeating our urgent appeal on the following dates: January 29, February 27, March 11, April 1, and April 5. On the same day, April 5, 1960, we received from His Beatitude a letter dated March 23, 1960, that he had received all our communications and has been trying his best to call a meeting of the Holy Synod to elect the bishop.[5]

Antony continued to press the patriarch to act on the election. "Again we wrote on April 8, April 30, and May 4."[6] Antony finally received a letter from the patriarch dated May 14, informing him that Metropolitan Elia Saleeby of Beirut would be coming to the United States for a personal visit. While here, he would "study the whole matter with us and report to His Beatitude upon his return, and that immediately upon his return the Synod [would] meet."[7]

Political Intrigue in Antioch

On May 24, 1960, His Eminence Metropolitan Elia Saleeby of Beirut, the special representative of the patriarch, arrived in the United States. Metropolitan Antony had several meetings with Saleeby. Antony believed that Saleeby "fully agreed that the solution of the Patriarchal

[4]*The Word* 4. 2 (February 1960): 20.
[5]*The Word* 4. 7 (September 1960): 15.
[6]Ibid.
[7]Ibid.

Council of November 1958 and May 1959, [was] the only way for our problem."[8] Saleeby promised, before leaving for Beirut, that he would submit his report to the patriarch and the Holy Synod immediately upon his return. Still, no final action on the part of the mother church was taken.

Growing ever more impatient with the Holy Synod's stalling, Antony wrote again on June 23 and July 6, appealing for a quick election by the Synod. On July 23, 1960, Antony received a letter informing him the Holy Synod would meet on July 25, two days later, to decide on the election of an auxiliary bishop for the Toledo diocese. Because of the short notice, Metropolitan Antony was unable to attend. Despite his absence, the meeting took place on July 26. Only six of the thirteen metropolitans met in Damascus: Epiphanius of Akkar, Niphon of Zahle, Alexander of Homs, Paul of Merjeyoun, Photius of Baghdad, and Gabriel of Ladikia. Their number was too few to establish the necessary canonical quorum, but they nonetheless decided to postpone the election of the bishop of Toledo and to dispatch Metropolitan Epiphanius of Akkar as patriarchal vicar to Toledo for six months. He was to study the problem and report to the patriarch.[9]

In the wake of the Damascus meeting, Metropolitan Ignatius Hurieky of Hama and Metropolitan Elias Moawd of Aleppo, together with leading members of the Patriarchal Council of Syria and Lebanon, immediately wired their protests to the patriarch. They asked him to stop this unlawful action against the holy canons and the Constitution of the Patriarchate. Upon receiving this request, His Beatitude ordered that the decisions of the Damascus meeting be nullified.

A cable was sent to Metropolitan Antony, dated August 2, 1960, that read: "Execution last meeting decision postponed. Letter follows. Patriarch Theodosius."[10] The letter that followed the telegram, also dated August 2, 1960, stated that the Holy Synod would meet on August 23, 1960, to elect a bishop for Toledo. Antony immediately

[8]Ibid.
[9]See *The Word* 4. 7 (September 1960): 15.
[10]Ibid.

replied to the patriarch, "requesting that he change the date of the meeting from August 23 to September 13 or 14 to allow us, and our brothers in Christ the Metropolitans of Argentina and Brazil, enough time to attend."[11] The patriarch agreed, and the meeting of the Synod was set for September 1960.

The "Shocking Uncanonical Visit"

In the meantime, contrary to the wishes of the Holy Synod, Metropolitan Epiphanius departed Lebanon for Toledo on August 17, 1960. After consulting with Lebanese authorities, the patriarch sent telegrams to American immigration authorities in Washington, D.C., New York, and Cleveland, Ohio, stating that "Metropolitan Epiphanius of the diocese of Akkar . . . secretly departed to USA, namely Toledo, Ohio, without our supreme authorization and in spite of our official warning . . . His presence in the USA and the Toledo diocese is absolutely illegal and prejudicial. Patriarch Theodosius."[12]

On August 20, 1960, Antony received a letter from the patriarch, in which the patriarch informed him that he expected him "to take all the necessary measures."[13] Immediately Antony sent a letter to the parishes of the Archdiocese of New York and all North America that said,

> In view of the disobedience of Metropolitan Epiphanius to the decision of the Holy Synod and the orders of His Beatitude the Patriarch, we feel it is our duty as the canonical shepherd of the North American Archdiocese to request of all our faithful clergy and laity in all North America to have nothing to do with this non-canonical visitor until he returns to [the] obedience of his mother church.[14]

[11]Ibid.
[12]Ibid., 16.
[13]Ibid.
[14]Ibid.

"We Have Reached the End of the Road"

Antony was preparing to depart for Beirut in a couple of weeks in order to participate in the Holy Synod's election of a bishop for Toledo. Knowing that Epiphanius might take advantage of his absence, he wrote a second letter on August 20, 1960, seeking to head off any ambush at the upcoming meeting of the Holy Synod. Antony knew discussions in the United States were futile. The problem was in the Holy Synod, and it was up to the Synod to solve it. There is a tone of urgency to his words:

> Now we have reached the end of the road . . . *It will be very wise if any number of our Trustees and leaders of the various parishes accompany us in this final trip.* For the last twenty-four years we have been struggling to keep the unity of our Archdiocese—not only for ourselves, but all our beloved people in North America. *Any division of this sacred unity is very harmful and will spread confusion everywhere. We must do all we can at this critical last hour to stop the evil hands working to divide us.* With the help of God and your loyal support we shall remain united.
>
> Our last request of all our beloved clergy and church organizations is NEVER TO ACCEPT IN THEIR CHURCHES OR IN THEIR PARISHES ANY CLERGYMAN OR ANY BISHOP—NO MATTER WHO [THEY] MAY BE—WITHOUT A SPECIAL LETTER SENT TO THEM UNDER OUR SIGNATURE AS THEIR LAWFUL AND CANONICAL BISHOP. This will keep our unity, and no troublemaker will ever be able to divide us against each other.[15]

But This Road Never Ends

Things did not go well in Beirut, however. The Toledo group had strong supporters on the Holy Synod who were able to stall proceedings by raising new objections to old decisions. It had become obvious that Antony needed to come to an agreement with the Toledo group if the archdiocese was to remain undivided.

[15]Ibid. Italicized emphasis added.

ANTONY BASHIR: METROPOLITAN & MISSIONARY

Although he had not received sufficient support to be named as one of the three candidates for bishop, Fr Michael Shaheen, pastor of St George Church in Montreal, Canada, began to emerge as the compromise candidate for bishop of Toledo. Certain individuals within the Toledo group launched a campaign in support of Shaheen becoming their new bishop.[16] While the Holy Synod continued to stall, secret negotiations between Fr Michael Shaheen and the Toledo people, led by Mary Douad, were also taking place. Some in Toledo, however, were adamantly opposed to Shaheen. They considered Shaheen, who had been ordained by Antony, as a puppet for Bashir. Fr Husson stated: "We do not want Shaheen; we want Ananias Kassab . . . Antony was just using Shaheen as a cover-up so that he could say that he had provided Toledo with a bishop. As you know, he was refused."[17]

A meeting was held at the Statler Hotel in Boston. In attendance were Fr Michael Shaheen, Fr Ilyas Kurban, John Khouri, Moussa Souaid, Monsour Laham, and Metropolitan Antony. Monsour Laham questioned Fr Michael as to the veracity of the rumors about his plans to become bishop of the Toledo group: "Is there truth to the fact that you have met with many individuals, and that this sort of thing has been promoted?" Fr Michael answered, "Yes!" "The man has candor at least; he did not deny it when I made these charges . . ."[18] (Laham's information came from Mary Douad, who was one of the participants in those negotiations.[19])

Sensing the wishes of the Toledo people and believing Shaheen might prove to be a workable solution to the problem, Metropolitan Antony sought to help make Shaheen acceptable to both factions of the Toledo group.

Nomination, Election, and Consecration

In spite of some opposition from a faction within the Toledo group, the decision was made to consecrate Fr Michael Shaheen as bishop of

[16]Monsour Laham, personal interview.
[17]Raphael Husson, personal interview.
[18]Monsour Laham, personal interview.
[19]Raphael Husson, personal interview.

Toledo and auxiliary to Metropolitan Antony. It had been almost two full years since the original nomination of three candidates to be the bishop of Toledo. On December 8, 1961, the General Council of the Patriarchate met and once again, after a lengthy debate, "finally decided that Toledo, Ohio, is not an archdiocese but an episcopate in the Archdiocese of New York and all North America with special status, as formerly decided (May 28, 1959)."[20] In further action, the General Council requested the patriarch "to take the necessary measures for the immediate nomination, election, and consecration of [the] bishop of Toledo."[21]

The next day, Metropolitan Antony explained the status of his archdiocese and his need for a bishop to assist him. "After reviewing all the past decisions and discussions relating to this question by both the Holy Synod and the General Council, it was decided that immediate steps be taken to facilitate the nomination, election, and consecration of a bishop of Toledo who shall have the right to commemorate in all Divine Services the names of both the Patriarch of Antioch and the Metropolitan of the Archdiocese."[22] Yet once again, even in making this decision, the Holy Synod sent a mixed message. Metropolitans normally commemorate the name of the patriarch and fellow metropolitans, while bishops commemorate the name of their metropolitan and their fellow bishops. By giving the right to commemorate the names of *both* patriarch and metropolitan to the new bishop of Toledo, they were arguably treating him as a metropolitan equal to the metropolitan of the archdiocese.

Three days later, on December 12, 1961, the Holy Synod met again, with the patriarch presiding, and decided the following:

1. The Rt Rev. Archimandrite Michael Shaheen, pastor of St George church, Montreal, Canada, is nominated and elected bishop of Toledo, in accordance with the above-mentioned decision of the Holy Synod.

---

[20]*The Word* 6. 1 (January 1962): 18.
[21]Ibid.
[22]Ibid.

2. His Beatitude the Patriarch is requested to notify [Fr Shaheen] and to make the necessary preparations with the Metropolitan of New York and all North America for the consecration of the new bishop.[23]

A Bishop without a Bishopric

Finally, a bishop for Toledo had been chosen. The January 1962 issue of *The Word* magazine, the official voice of the archdiocese, announced the election of Shaheen as a bishop "to assist his Eminence, the Metropolitan of the Archdiocese of New York and all North America, in all matters pertaining to the general administration of the Archdiocese, as defined by the Metropolitan."[24]

That same issue, under the bold heading "THE NEW BISHOP ELECT," sought to redefine Shaheen's duties as assistant to Metropolitan Antony, rather than as a bishop of a diocese within the archdiocese:

> It was the unanimous decision of the Holy Synod of the Patriarchate of Antioch in their two meetings, December 9 and 11, 1961, that the newly elected bishop shall assist the metropolitan of the Archdiocese in the general administration of the Archdiocese. He will have the title of bishop of Toledo, and his duties will be all over the Archdiocese. He will not be a bishop of one group in the Archdiocese. The Holy Synod's plans are to help keep the Archdiocese united to be able to maintain its progress. It is the sacred duty of every loyal member of our North American Church to abide by this wise plan and help the hierarchy in its enforcement.[25]

This redefining of the role of the bishop of Toledo was a significant change. Hitherto mention had always been made of establishing "a bishopric under the Archdiocese of New York and all North America, in the name of Toledo, Ohio and Dependencies, with the understanding that this bishopric will have geographic boundaries, and its bishop

[23]Ibid.
[24]*The Word* 6. 3 (March 1962): 20.
[25]*The Word* 6. 1 (January 1962): 18.

will be under the jurisdiction of the Metropolitan."[26] With this new definition however, it seemed that the bishop of Toledo would be a bishop at large with no association with a specific see. He would in fact be a bishop without a bishopric. It was yet to be seen what the Toledo group would have to say about these efforts to eliminate the bishopric of Toledo by disassociating their bishop from his see.

Bargaining with the Toledo Group

Bishop-elect Shaheen met with the Toledo group to discuss his role as the new bishop. The Toledo leaders told Shaheen that two things had to be done before they would accept him: firstly, the consecration would have to be done in Damascus; and secondly, they would maintain their own treasury in Toledo, to take care of the Bishop's financial needs.[27] When Antony refused to agree to these demands, Shaheen told him the Toledo group would not do it any other way. Shaheen continued to insist that Toledo's offer be accepted. Finally, after several weeks, Antony acceded to Toledo's request.[28]

Your Presence Extremely Necessary

On January 30, 1962, Antony received a telegram from the patriarch of Antioch: "Your presence with Reverend Shaheen extremely necessary. General Council will meet 9 February and Holy Synod 10 February. Please cable date of arrival."[29] Metropolitan Antony and Fr Shaheen departed for Damascus on February 6.

On the following Sunday, February 11, at the Church of the Holy Cross in Damascus, Archimandrite Michael was consecrated bishop of Toledo. At the same time, another election took place. Archimandrite Ilyas Kurban, former pastor of St George Church in Boston, Massachusetts, was elected the metropolitan archbishop of Tripoli, Al-Koura and Dependencies in Lebanon. It was an ironic turn of

[26]*The Word* 3. 9 (November 1959): 17.
[27]*The Word* 6. 11 (November 1962): 11.
[28]Ibid.
[29]*The Word* 6. 3 (March 1962): 20.

events. Kurban, who had received the most votes in the Toledo election, now became metropolitan-elect for Tripoli, and Shaheen, who had received the least, was now consecrated bishop of Toledo.

Patriarch Theodosius VI officially announced the consecration of Archimandrite Michael Shaheen as the new bishop of Toledo in a letter dated Monday, February 12, 1962.

> We are happy to inform you that at the request of our most beloved brother Antony, the Metropolitan of New York and all North America, the Holy Synod of Antioch, in its session held at the Patriarchate in Damascus, Syria, on Tuesday, December 12, 1961, elected our spiritual son Archimandrite Michael Shaheen a bishop, with the title of bishop of Toledo, Ohio, to assist His Eminence the Metropolitan of the Archdiocese of New York and all North America, in all matters pertaining to the general administration of the Archdiocese—as defined by the Metropolitan. In all divine services performed by the new bishop he must commemorate the names of the Patriarch and the Metropolitan of the Archdiocese.
>
> In accordance with this decision of the Holy Synod, His Eminence Metropolitan Antony was requested to come to Damascus with the bishop-elect for the consecration services. On Sunday morning, February 11, 1962, with the help of Almighty God and the assistance of the most reverend members of the Holy Synod, during the Divine Liturgy at the church of the Holy and Life-Giving Cross at Damascus, Syria, we consecrated the new bishop.[30]

[30]Ibid.

CHAPTER 8

Antony and Michael

Upon their return, Bishop Michael "tried several times to establish himself in Toledo, but was repeatedly refused by the group."[1] Fr Husson stated the Toledo position bluntly: "In the first place, we do not want Michael; I told [Antony], 'He is not for us. You used Michael as a cover up to solve your problem.'"[2] In the meantime, Michael continued to serve his former parish in Montreal, "where he continued receiving his monthly salary plus over $3,000 worth of gifts, such as vestments, etc."[3]

Toledo knew that if they accepted Michael, their diocese was dead. His title might be bishop of Toledo, but Michael's duties had nothing to do with the administration of the bishopric of Toledo. Instead, his duties were to assist the Metropolitan of the Archdiocese of New York "in all matters pertaining to the general administration of the Archdiocese—as defined by the metropolitan."[4] For this reason, the Toledo group refused to accept Michael as their bishop.

Because of her wealth, power, and support from others, Mary Douad had been instrumental in choosing Michael Shaheen to be the spiritual leader of the Toledo diocese. The Toledo group eventually decided upon a two-pronged course of action. First, they decided that they would in fact accept Michael, but only if he refused to cooperate with Antony. Secondly, they planned to request a bishop from the old country to serve them. Behind the scenes the Toledo group took steps to implement both courses of action.

[1] *The Word* 6. 11 (November 1962): 11.
[2] Raphael Husson., personal interview
[3] *The Word* 6. 11 (November 1962): 11.
[4] *The Word* 6. 3 (March 1962): 20.

In the midst of the uncertainty about Bishop Michael's acceptance, there arose rumors that he had reached an arrangement with Toledo in which he agreed to denounce Metropolitan Antony and proclaim his independence, in accordance with the wishes of those who held control over Toledo. In response to these rumors, a meeting was held in Montreal. At this meeting, Bishop Michael declared: "I belong to this Archdiocese, but I want an opportunity. I would like you to allow me to go to meet with the Toledo churches and try to convince them, since I am named the Bishop of Toledo, to be within the fold of the Archdiocese. On my honor, as God is my judge, I will not try to do anything otherwise but will try to bring them back where they belong—with us."[5]

In early May 1962, Michael and Fr Raphael of Charleston notified Antony "that they had a meeting of the [Toledo] Group, and that the decision was not to allow [Michael] to mention [Antony's] name in their churches."[6] Also repeated was "their previous request that they would like to have *their own treasury to pay the bishop* . . . "[7] As these events were transpiring, Metropolitan Antony attempted to maintain peace within the archdiocese at all costs. Repeatedly the Toledo group had requested "to have their own treasury, to pay the bishop, and not to live on charity . . . and not to mention Metropolitan Antony in their church."[8]

Metropolitan Antony agreed to these requests, but Bishop Michael and Fr Raphael questioned whether the Archdiocese Board of Trustees would concur. Antony reported: "They insisted that I call a special meeting of the Archdiocese board to approve this. For the sake of preserving unity and peace, I called a special meeting of the Archdiocese board. We met in Montreal on the 18th and 19th of May, 1962, and unanimously decided to grant their request, with the understanding that the *Archdiocese remains united*."[9] Also at this meeting, Bishop Michael again solemnly pledged that he would always "sup-

[5]Monsour Laham, personal interview.
[6]*The Word* 6. 11 (November 1962): 11.
[7]Ibid.
[8]Ibid.
[9]Ibid.

port the unity of the Archdiocese and would never separate himself from the Archdiocese."[10]

At the Archdiocese Board of Trustees meeting on May 18 and 19, 1962, Metropolitan Antony reported that Bishop Michael of Toledo had not been able to start his pastoral duties on account of "various difficulties." He suggested that Bishop Michael be "authorized to use his judgment in dealing with the obstacles and to do all he can to please our beloved brethren of Toledo, assuring them that all we want is to see them happy, enjoying peace and harmony with their bishop for the glory of God and the continuation of peace and love among our people."[11] The board expressed its satisfaction with this plan, and Bishop Michael expressed his sincere thanks, pledging to do his best. Having been given permission by the board of trustees "to use his judgment," and to "do all he can to please," Michael could now enter into negotiations with Toledo and find out what their conditions were for accepting him as their bishop.

Surprise Move in Antioch

Less than a week after the Archdiocese Board of Trustees meeting, the Holy Synod of Antioch met on May 24, 1962. Once again, they discussed the problem of Toledo.[12] The pro-Toledo faction of the Holy Synod came prepared with a motion, carefully thought out and logically presented, in defense of Toledo as an independent diocese.

The motion first addressed the problems Michael faced: "After careful study of the Toledo, Ohio, problem, it appeared that the last decision of the Holy Synod in respect to this matter was not executed, and that the bishop elected by the Holy Synod for its pastoral care was unable to perform his duties there."[13] Next, it spoke of Michael's inability to perform his duties, and the need for them to make a complete re-examination of the Toledo situation from its very inception.

[10]Ibid.
[11]*The Word* 6. 9 (September 1962): 17.
[12]Ibid.
[13]Ibid.

A careful search was made of all the records and decisions of the Antiochian Holy Synod respecting this subject, from the very beginning of the Toledo problem; nothing was found to indicate the establishment of Toledo as an independent diocese *de jure* (legally), but it was found to exist *de facto* (in fact), and there was discovered in the decisions of the Holy Synod an indication of the existence of a Metropolitan there as an active member of the Holy Synod, having all of the rights and duties of the other Metropolitans of the Antiochian Patriarchate.[14]

In other words, Samuel David, who was the former bishop of Toledo, had in fact been a metropolitan and a voting member of the Holy Synod of Antioch, and this set an important precedent.

Thirdly, the motion noted that documents existed that referred to both Toledo and New York as archdioceses. In particular, the original draft of the constitution of the Antiochian Patriarchate, which had been signed by all the members of the Orthodox General Congress held at Damascus, on November 18, 1955—including the majority of the metropolitans of the Patriarchate and the majority of the members of the congress authorized to frame constitutions and establish new dioceses—had listed both New York and Toledo as archdioceses.

In addition, at the time when the draft of the constitution was being discussed in 1955, the late Patriarch Alexander objected to the printing of the constitution unless the name of the diocese of Toledo was erased from the list of the dioceses of the Patriarchate. He feared that including the name of Toledo in the list would cause confusion among the faithful of North America. The committee that was in charge of printing the constitution was requested by the patriarch to solve this problem by simply replacing the reference in the document to both dioceses with the following notice: "NORTH AMERICA WILL BE DISCUSSED BY THE GENERAL COUNCIL." As a result, the original draft of the constitution, the one that was signed, included the name of Toledo in the list of dioceses; but the copies of the constitution that were printed for distribution had the names of both New York and Toledo omitted.

[14]Ibid.

Based on these four reasons, the pro-Toledo faction moved that the Patriarchate "go back to the original draft of the Constitution as it was approved by the General Congress before it was printed, and to re-record Toledo, Ohio, among the independent dioceses of the Antiochian Patriarchate."[15] A majority of the metropolitans present agreed, and the motion passed. In a surprise move in Antioch, the diocese of Toledo had been reborn.

Antony Protests the Decision

A copy of the decisions of this meeting reached Metropolitan Antony in the first week of July. His response was swift and to the point. His letter contained the following protest:

1. In the invitation we received to attend this session of the Holy Synod, the Toledo problem was not included in the agenda, and therefore I replied that I could not attend. For this reason, we protest against this action taken in our absence without giving us an opportunity to defend our rights, and we cannot be responsible for any decision taken without warning in our absence. When our representative in the General Council, as appears from your minutes, requested this problem be discussed in the Council, he was refused that right on the grounds that the subject was not included in the council's agenda. Why then was it discussed in the Holy Synod although it was not on the agenda of that body? And then a like discussion was not permitted in the General Council meeting because it was not included in the agenda there? Where is the logic or justice in this puzzle?

2. We notice in the minutes of the General Council held on May 26 that the decisions taken in the December meeting of the Council were read and approved by all the metropolitans and delegates in attendance. The December meeting decided, "*That Toledo is not an independent diocese, it is only an episcopate*

[15]Ibid.

in the Archdiocese of New York and all North America." Does this mean that your Synod at the same time blesses and curses the same object? Or what does it mean, if anything?

3. On behalf of all our people in North America, we are convinced that this decision is contrary to the fundamental laws and sacred canons of our holy Orthodox Church, which strictly prohibit setting up a diocese within a diocese.

4. Your reference to the original draft of the constitution of the Patriarchate before it was printed, "that the name of Toledo was in it, and that the patriarch erased it . . . etc." and that "North America will be discussed by the General Council in accordance with the Constitution of 1955"—this is against you and not with you. The General Council did meet and did carefully discuss the North American problem in 1958, and again 1959, and again 1961, and unanimously decided that Toledo is not an independent diocese but is an episcopate in the Archdiocese of New York and all North America. And in accordance with all these decisions the Holy Synod met in December 1961, and elected the bishop of Toledo to assist in the Archdiocese of North America.

5. Regarding your statement that after checking all the records of the Patriarchate of Antioch and the decisions of the Holy Synod you were not able to find anything to show the legal existence of an independent diocese of Toledo, Ohio, and your further statement that in spite of your admission of the illegality of this diocese, you still want to recognize it—to all of this, we refuse to respond at all, because we find it A STRANGE WONDER. No one can tell the *real causes* that led to it, but He whose eyes never sleep, He alone will judge every man according to his heart's intention.

6. For all of the above reasons, we refuse to accept this decision, and reserve to ourselves and to our Archdiocese the right to protect and preserve the unity, peace, and progress of our Archdiocese.

Meanwhile, our relations with our beloved brethren of Toledo, Ohio, will be determined by ourselves in the proper manner, mutually acceptable and beneficial to both of us, without ever having to face again the same paradoxical treatment and decisions that have no other aim than to create confusion, hatred, and division among our people in North America.

May the suffering Lord and Savior Jesus Christ help save our church from its suffering because of the sins of many of us.[16]

Another "Shocking Tragedy" from the Old Country

Antony tried to get in touch with Michael "to remind him of his sacred pledge to defend the unity of the Archdiocese."[17] But Michael could not be located. He was, in fact, not even in America. A few weeks after the Archdiocese Board of Trustees meeting in Montreal, the archdiocese was notified that Bishop Michael had left for Syria, accompanied by Miss Mary Douad and other representatives of the Toledo group. Upon their return, Bishop Michael claimed that he had been made archbishop and metropolitan, and appointed head of an independent Archdiocese of Toledo.

Rumors of these events quickly reached Metropolitan Antony. He could hardly believe what was happening. As a rule, he trusted his clergy and had no fear of disturbances or betrayal, so he was shocked to discover that one of his pastors was trying to betray him.

We were informed that he went to Syria secretly and without our knowledge. We were shocked later on, to learn that he returned to America *claiming that he was made an Archbishop . . . and a Metropolitan . . . and the head of an independent Archdiocese of Toledo* . . . There was nothing to do at the time but wait for the General Convention to meet in August at Asbury Park in New Jersey, to decide our official stand regarding this most shocking tragedy.[18]

[16]Ibid., 17–18.
[17]*The Word* 6. 11 (November 1962): 11.
[18]Ibid.

An Angry Archdiocese Fights Back

The Seventh Annual Archdiocesan Convention met on August 21–26, 1962, at Asbury Park. In no uncertain terms, the archdiocese unanimously fought back against the May 1962 decision of the Holy Synod of Antioch. During the convention the clergy of the archdiocese, in a show of strength, unity, and solidarity, took their stand with Metropolitan Antony. Fr. Ellis Khouri, Protosyngellos and Dean of the Clergy, presented the following pledge to Antony, signed by more than one hundred priests:

> In view of recent events which have taken place in our church which threaten the unity of the Syrian Antiochian Church of North America, we the undersigned priests present this document, endorsed by us personally and individually, as a testament and reaffirmation of our continued loyalty to our outstanding and incomparable archepiscopal leader and spiritual father, Metropolitan Antony Bashir.
>
> Be it known to all men that we are his sons and he is our archpastor, and to him we submit ourselves obediently, devotedly, and with filial piety, which obedience, devotion, and submission we render to no other man.
>
> May the Lord Jesus Christ, our great High Priest, and the lover of truth, seal this pledge for all time and keep us steadfast in our faith with purity and honor. And may He who is the great Shepherd of the Church preserve our Most Reverend Metropolitan Antony and protect him and grant him many years.[19]

The clergy then presented Metropolitan Antony with a copy of a cablegram that had been sent to the patriarch, the Holy Synod, and the General Council of the Patriarchate. Authenticated copies were mailed to the patriarch and to every member of the Holy Synod and the General Council.[20]

We, the undersigned clergy of the Archdiocese of New York and all North America, assembled at the Seventh Annual Archdioce-

[19]*The Word* 6. 10 (October 1962): 14.
[20]Ibid.

san Convention at Asbury, New Jersey, August 21 through August 26, 1962, do strongly protest the non-canonical decision made in May of this year, which threatens the unity of this Archdiocese and which has created a great deal of unrest among our people. With one heart and with one faith we reaffirm our loyalty to the Most Reverend Metropolitan Antony Bashir, praying to God, who has saved us by His Precious Blood, to enlighten you to reconsider that irregular decision so that the dignity of the holy local and Ecumenical Councils might be preserved. Your hasty decision jeopardizes our relationship with you and threatens the well-being of the flock.

The clergy and the laity who have, by their sweat and blood, built this flourishing Antiochian Archdiocese are extremely anxious about the future destiny of the Antiochian Church as a whole in these times of great stress. We shall not be completely content until we receive from you, as most holy fathers, reassurance of your watchful concern for the sanctity of the Holy Canons and the dignity and welfare of the whole church.

May the truth, which has freed us from the bondage of sin, help us to remain *One Flock* under *One Shepherd* in the *One Christ,* Jesus our Savior.

Not only the clergy but the laity as well protested the May decision. Nicholas Hamaty, president of the North American Council of SOYO, along with his executive board and the other SOYO delegates at the convention, presented a signed resolution taking their stand with Metropolitan Antony:

The North American Council of SOYO unanimously endorses the position taken by Metropolitan Antony Bashir during the past 26 years in his unfailing faith and devotion to his God and to his flock, to achieve the present success in stemming any tide which has been a threat to the unity of the Syrian Antiochian Archdiocese of North America.[21]

[21]Ibid.

The most dramatic and extraordinary event occurred when the General Assembly of the Convention voted unanimously on August 24 to send a *Resolution of Protest* to the Holy Synod. Their protest came three months to the day that the Holy Synod had made its "irregular" decision. It is also of some note that a *Resolution of Protest* was drafted and submitted by the Board of Trustees of the St Elias parish of Toledo, Ohio. The Resolution of Protest was signed "by each and every Delegate in Convention Assembled"[22] and read as follows

> Protesting the action of the Holy Synod of Antioch dated May 24, 1962, at Damascus—
>
> WHEREAS, the Archdiocese of New York and all North America has continuously existed DE JURE, and
>
> WHEREAS, the said Archdiocese has always respected and obeyed the canonical decision of the Patriarchate of which it is a part and wishes to continue so, and
>
> WHEREAS, the subject of the Archdiocese within an Archdiocese was properly and canonically resolved in December of 1961 by the Holy Synod of Antioch, and
>
> WHEREAS, this Archdiocese in Convention assembled on August 22 through August 26, 1962, has determined officially that the decision of the Holy Synod of May 24, 1962, *is improper, non-canonical and detrimental to the best interests of The Syrian Antiochian Orthodox Archdiocese of New York and all North America, and that this Archdiocese can neither respect nor agree to be bound by this non-canonical act,*
>
> THEREFORE, be it resolved that this Archdiocese through its lay delegates and parishes protests against this decision and deplores it as non-canonical and not binding upon this Archdiocese, and further requests that the Holy Synod reconsider the decision of May 24, 1962, and be it further resolved that all delegates in this Convention shall sign this resolution for and on behalf of their parishes and shall transmit a copy of same to His Beatitude the Patriarch and to each member of the Holy Synod and members of Mixed Council of the Patriarchate of Antioch.[23]

[22]Ibid.
[23]Ibid., 14–15.

Having gone on record as standing with Antony against the decision of the Holy Synod, the board of trustees, clergy, and lay delegates of the convention then took steps to define a position regarding any parishes in the Toledo group who had separated themselves from the archdiocese. They agreed unanimously upon the following:

Notwithstanding any divisive and non-canonical decisions of the Holy Synod, the Board and the Archdiocese hereby declare that with God's blessing we shall maintain the spiritual good health and the continued progress of the Archdiocese of New York and all North America under the respected and enlightened leadership of our beloved Metropolitan Antony. Meanwhile, the Archdiocese shall continue its request to have the Holy Synod review its May decision, and to maintain, at the same time, full right to appeal its case to a higher ecclesiastical court in the future. All relations with the Toledo group who separated themselves from unity with the Archdiocese must cease until they reunite themselves with the Archdiocese.[24]

Having taken a stand together in solidarity, as a completely united convention behind their metropolitan, the Archdiocese Board of Trustees cabled the following official protest:

WHEREAS Metropolitan Antony was canonically consecrated in April of 1936 as Archbishop of the one and only canonical Archdiocese of New York and North America with the Antiochian Jurisdiction,

WHEREAS the Antiochian Holy Synod again and again, and at its most recent meeting of December 1961, again reaffirmed the above decision, as the only canonical Archdiocese in North America,

WHEREAS Metropolitan Antony Bashir, his Clergy, and his Laity have always complied with all canonical and legal decisions of the Antiochian Holy Synod these many years,

THEREFORE be it resolved, that the Board of Trustees on behalf of all the clergy and laity of the Archdiocese of New York

[24]Ibid., 15.

and North America violently abhor and object to the non-canonical decision made by the Holy Antiochian Synod at its meeting of May 24, 1962, and emphatically state that we will never accept or abide by any and all non-canonical and illegal decisions made by it, and hold those members who voted for it responsible for the disturbance of the welfare of our Archdiocese and the entire Antiochian Church.[25]

The Great Divorce

For over twenty-five years, since the time of his consecration, Metropolitan Antony's life had been filled with attempts at reconciliation with the Toledo group. During this time, decisions were made and rulings enforced for the sake of having one united Church. All attempts by the archdiocese, however, had thus far been in vain. Indeed, this problem would not be resolved in Antony's lifetime.

Unable to tolerate these petty quarrels any longer, Antony issued an edict to all churches stating that there was now "a total suspension with the Toledo group and whosoever supports Toledo's position . . . They wanted to be independent: let them be independent."[26] The priests and parishioners of the archdiocese had grown frustrated and disillusioned, and had lost all confidence in the Holy Synod. Even priests who were under the Toledo diocese were dissatisfied with the decision to elevate Bishop Michael to metropolitan. Fr Michael Howard was one of those who demonstrated his concern for and obedience to the truth; for the sake of peace and unity, he left the Toledo diocese and joined Metropolitan Antony.

The creation of an archdiocese within an archdiocese was unthinkable. It provoked one protest after another. People lost confidence in their leaders. Personal pride and personal gain filled the hearts of those who had perpetrated this fraud. The faithful could only pray that one day the simony and betrayal would be stopped. To Miss Mary Douad, now long since deceased, must be given much of the credit for adding to the friction, since she worked tirelessly for the

[25]Ibid.
[26]Ibid., 17.

proclamation of the independent Archdiocese of Toledo. Metropolitan Antony would not live long enough to see his dream of one united archdiocese come to pass.

What Went Wrong in Antioch?

At the May 24 meeting of the Holy Synod, two of the metropolitans had voted against the division, two had abstained, and six had voted to ignore the Synod's previous decisions. Why did the Holy Synod behave this way? Did Mary Douad have enough money to buy a metropolitanship for Shaheen? No one knows. "But he who never sleeps . . . will reward everyone according to his heart's intentions."[27] In the *Los Angeles Times,* Mary Douad was referred to as "the rich woman member of the Holy Synod who was called to mediate the crisis in the Church of Antioch."[28] When Protosyngellos Ellis Khouri learned that she was present with the archbishops in the grand salon, while the official delegation was in the other room, he protested to the patriarch and asked that she be made to leave. It was suggested that she had been interfering in church politics for years, based on her role as a major financial contributor to the bishops and institutions of the Patriarchate.

A Footnote to History

Metropolitan Antony steadfastly rejected a divided archdiocese. "We will not accept division" became his battle cry.[29] He died on February 15, 1966, still believing in unity. He also died feeling betrayed by Bishop Michael Shaheen. After Antony's death, Fr Philip Saliba was elected and consecrated as Antony's successor, becoming Metropolitan of the Archdiocese of New York and all North America. Nine years later, on June 24, 1975, Metropolitan Philip and Metropolitan Michael signed *Articles of Reunification* that restored administrative

[27]Ibid.
[28]Antony Gabriel, *The Ancient Church on New Shores: Antioch in North America* (San Bernardino, CA: St. Willibord's Press, 1996), 128.
[29]*The Word* 6. 11 (November 1962): 17.

unity among all the Antiochian Orthodox Christians in North America. This document was in turn presented to the Holy Synod, which ratified it on August 19, 1975. In doing so, the Synod recognized Philip as the metropolitan primate and Michael as an auxiliary archbishop.

Archbishop Michael served as a bishop for thirty years, thirteen of them as bishop of an independent Archdiocese of Toledo, and the last seventeen years as auxiliary archbishop of a united Antiochian Archdiocese of North America. In an ironic turn of events, the man chosen by Antony to bring unity became instrumental in bringing about disunity instead. Yet he was also responsible in the end, along with Metropolitan Philip, for finally achieving the unity for which Antony so desperately fought.

The Toledo group did not like Antony, and they rejected him personally. But once Antony had passed away, when the time was right, Archbishop Michael was able to return Toledo to the fold of a united Antiochian Archdiocese.

CHAPTER 9

Antony as Archpastor

In 1936, the Archdiocese of New York and all North America consisted of approximately thirty churches scattered throughout the country. Fearing that these churches might lose their identification with the faith and the mother church, Metropolitan Antony took on the task of visiting from city to city in hopes of preserving unity and establishing new missions in America. By 1961, forty-nine new churches had been founded or new buildings acquired, and forty-nine new parish rectories with sixteen church halls had been added. All of these were financially sound, and many were in the process of expansion. During his almost thirty years as metropolitan, Antony "molded the Archdiocese into a tightly knit organization, [that was] efficiently and democratically organized on regional and international levels, to serve its many communities."[1]

The Transition from Arabic to English

Knowing that the second, third, and following generations would not be able to understand the use of Arabic in the Divine Liturgy, Antony devoted his life to meeting the challenge of making the transition from Arabic to English. He was a man of vision and insight, and he knew that it would take time for translations to be completed. He understood that the church had to begin the work of translating now in order to have English texts ready for the coming generations. He prepared the archdiocese for this transition by translating and publishing in English more than thirty books on Orthodox history, doctrine, tradition, prayer, and music. He introduced the first all-English liturgy to

[1]Salem, *Metropolitan Antony Bashir*, 15.

be used anywhere. He laid down plans for a Sunday school program and provided appropriate English-language educational materials. He began the schooling of the first American-born young men for the clergy and ordained many of them to the priesthood. He established and published *The Word* magazine as the first English-language Archdiocesan journal in America. In short, he spearheaded the "Americanization" of his church and set an example that other Orthodox ethnic groups could follow.

Looking for a Few Good Men

Antony not only needed English texts to accomplish the transition from Arabic to English, but also clergy who shared his vision of making this transition a reality. He immediately began recruiting seminarians and pastors from the mother church of Antioch who were qualified to serve in both English and Arabic. He also warmly accepted convert clergy prepared to serve Orthodox parishes in the English language. At times, he even accepted some clergy who were considered "undesirables" in the denominations from which they came, "in his desperation to find priests to serve the Church."[2]

Neither Metropolitan Antony nor the Archdiocesan clergy ever resented non-Arab priests, including those who were converts. Arab Christians quickly became citizens of the countries to which they emigrated, and tended to assimilate rapidly to their new culture. There were, of course, exceptions. On one occasion, an elderly priest wrote a letter to a parish board in an attempt to arouse feelings against non-Arab clergy. But such cases were extremely rare. Non-Arab and convert clergy were not criticized on the basis of nationality, but only for the same reasons that Arab clergy were criticized: for being failures as priests. Fathers Schneirla, Upson, Buben, Prieston, Abboud, Zakah, and Moses were among those accepted without any discrimination whatsoever.[3] Metropolitan Antony and the archdiocese welcomed all clergy, regardless of their origin,, on the basis of their love for God and their manifest willingness to serve faithfully the archdiocese.

[2]Schneirla, personal interview.
[3]Ibid.

An Orthodox Seminary for America

As the archdiocese grew, laymen began searching for educated clergy who could enlighten them on the finer points of Orthodox faith and tradition. Metropolitan Antony wanted his clergy to be molded in the faith and capable of proclaiming it to the world. In order to achieve this goal, he encouraged young American-born men to enter the seminaries with which he associated himself. He realized that, without educated clergy, many communities would lose interest in the faith and begin to disperse. Without proper education, Orthodoxy could not grow and become recognized in America.

At first, most young seminarians from the archdiocese enrolled at Holy Cross Seminary in Brookline, Massachusetts. Founded by the Greek Orthodox Archdiocese, Holy Cross Seminary has as its primary purpose the education of priests in the Orthodox faith. As a Greek seminary, however, its secondary purpose was the transmission of Hellenic culture. In the 1950s, Antony began sending Antiochian seminarians to St Vladimir's Orthodox Seminary in New York, for he "recognized that the team which organized St Vladimir's, or at least took it over in the early fifties, was the nucleus of an American Orthodox reality."[4] Very much impressed with the seminary's leadership, faculty, and theological curriculum, which was offered in English, Antony believed that St Vladimir's was intended not to serve as an ethnic seminary, but simply as an Orthodox one. At the Seminary Jubilee in 1958, Metropolitan Antony discouraged "the promotion of any nationalist school other than a truly American school, stressing that only in this way can an American Orthodox Church be finally established."[5]

Antony not only paid the costs of tuition, room, board, and books for the seminarians, but also supported the seminary morally and financially. On October 17, 1964, at the dedication of the educational building constructed at the seminary's new home in Crestwood, New York, Metropolitan Antony pledged a total of $30,000 on behalf of

[4]From a personal interview with Rev. Alexander Schmemann, the dean of St Vladimir's Orthodox Seminary, held on May 1, 1972 in Scarsdale, NY.

[5]*The Word* 2.12 (December 1958): 18.

himself and personal contributors from the Antiochian Archdiocese. A seminary building fund was established to support and assist the seminary. The continuation of this pledge was further encouraged by Antony's successor, Metropolitan Philip Saliba.

An Orthodox Seminary for Lebanon

As much as Metropolitan Antony dedicated his life to the Church in America, he was also dedicated to the mother church. He dreamed of educating young seminarians for the Patriarchate of Antioch. For many years, Antioch had dreamed of building a theological academy in Lebanon in order to generate a spiritual renaissance in the Middle East. "Metropolitan Antony realized that the spiritual leaders of the Church of Antioch must study theology in their own country and that a greater emphasis must be placed in preserving the historic mission of Antioch."[6]

In the early sixties, Metropolitan Antony made a personal pledge of $250,000, on behalf of the Antiochian Archdiocese, for the establishment of just such a theological academy. He did not live long enough to see his dream fulfilled. However, on August 15, 1966, one day after the consecration of Metropolitan Philip Saliba, the groundbreaking for the Academy of St John of Damascus took place at the Balamand. Attending the ceremony were Patriarch Theodosius, the newly consecrated Metropolitan Philip, and many other high-ranking religious and political dignitaries.

Once opened, the Academy achieved a place of prominence in the Orthodox sphere of the Middle East. Its dean, Metropolitan Ignatius Hazim, was elected patriarch in 1979, as Ignatius IV. These events, however, were not yet on the horizon on that August day in 1966. No one could anticipate that Elias IV would sit on the patriarchal throne following the death of Patriarch Theodosius in 1970, or that Ignatius would ascend to that same throne upon the death of Elias IV.

Metropolitan Antony did not live to see any of these events, but he believed in the future of the Antiochian Church. He knew that future required an educated and theologically trained clergy, not only in

[6]Paul W. Schneirla, *The Word* 15. 10 (December 1971): 5.

America, but also in the Patriarchate at large. Bashir was a man of vision, but he was no idle dreamer. He raised the money and pointed the way. The last chapter has not yet been written on the many achievements that will ultimately be built upon the foundations laid by Metropolitan Antony Bashir.

Organizing the Youth of the Archdiocese

From the beginning of his tenure, Metropolitan Antony supported those who saw a need for a national organization of Orthodox youth in America. Through the efforts of a small group of Syrian-Lebanese Orthodox communities in New England, headed by the energetic Charles T. Hyder of Lawrence, Massachusetts, an organization called "The Federation of Syrian Orthodox Youth" was created. Bashir gave his blessing to this endeavor. In 1939, this organization took a new name, "The Orthodox Catholic Frontier."[7]

The Orthodox Catholic Frontier tackled many problems, finding solutions to most and laying a foundation for greater youth work to begin. For example, the first Orthodox Sunday school lesson series in English was created and distributed. Music for the Divine Liturgy and for other services was written in Western notation and made available to church choirs. These musical arrangements preserved the Byzantine melodies while replacing the original notation with the system used in the West. Choir festivals were held in which various church choirs presented the liturgical music of the Orthodox Church in concert form. The *Orthodox American* was the first youth magazine to be introduced within the Antiochian Archdiocese. Through this publication, many young men and women who served in the armed forces during the Second World War were able to stay in contact with the life of the archdiocese. Last but not least, a seminary fund for the training of future priests was established.

The success of the Orthodox Catholic Frontier in New England spurred Metropolitan Antony to encourage other regions to join this fellowship. With the blessing of the metropolitan, Mr Hyder and the New England chapters formed a national youth organization. Several

[7]Charles T. Hyder, *History of New England S.O.Y.O* (Lawrence, MA: 1963).

regional groups of Orthodox youth met in 1951 to create the North American Council of Syrian Orthodox Youth Organizations, with the abbreviated, "euphonious" name of SOYO.[8]

SOYO played a critical role in reaching the second and third generations raised in America. As the foremost religious organization focused on the spiritual growth and unity of the youth within the archdiocese, SOYO enlarged young people's knowledge of Church affairs and widened their Orthodox horizons and viewpoints. It deepened their understanding of the Orthodox Church and stimulated solidarity and loyalty. SOYO promoted the highest ideals of the Orthodox faith. Through its activities, it provided many opportunities for the youth of the archdiocese to live the charitable, social, and religious life of the Church.

Working for National Recognition for the Church

Metropolitan Antony's charismatic leadership was not simply directed toward his own flock. He was also concerned with other Orthodox national jurisdictions in North America. He dreamed of a united American Orthodox Church that would foster public recognition of Orthodoxy as the fourth major faith in North America. Antony knew that only by being united would the Orthodox Church become large enough to rank with Protestantism, Catholicism, and Judaism in the mind of the general public.

Antony worked untiringly for unity by cooperating with his fellow Orthodox hierarchs. He was instrumental in the movement that led to the "Eastern Orthodox" (E.O.) stamp on the identification tags of men and women in the armed forces. He labored for the official recognition of the Orthodox faith by Congress and state legislatures. Courtesies and honors were bestowed upon Archbishop Antony at the request of Representative Virginia E. Jeckes, a member of the House of Representatives from Indiana, and by the Rev. James Stera Montgomery, the chaplain of the House.[9] Through their efforts, an historic

---

[8]Ibid.

[9]Antony Bashir, *Letter to the Parishes of the Archdiocese* dated February 18, 1937.

day for the American Orthodox people came to pass on February 18, 1937, when Metropolitan Antony became the first Orthodox archbishop to open with prayer a session of the United States House of Representatives.

Antony's efforts to establish himself as a visible presence led to his warm and personal friendship with President Franklin Roosevelt. On several occasions, the prelate was the president's guest at the White House. When they first met, President Roosevelt reportedly joked, "I notice that your title covers New York and all of North America. Your territory is bigger than mine." To which Antony replied, "Not only that, but I serve for more terms."[10]

Metropolitan Antony also participated in the larger world of ecclesiastical affairs. He represented the Patriarchate of Antioch at the United Christian Conference on Life and Work at Edinburgh, Scotland, in 1938. In the same year, he was also a delegate to the World Conference on Faith and Order at Oxford, England.

Working for Orthodox Jurisdictional Unity

Anthony Bashir always opposed isolationism. He believed in going outside the ethnic community and making himself known to the world for the purpose of promoting the Orthodox faith and the unity of all mankind. The unity of the Orthodox faith was forever his vision. He realized that the many separate Orthodox groups such as the Greeks, Russians, Romanians, Serbs, and Antiochians had to cooperate if they were to achieve their common hopes. In the end, he wanted one united Orthodox Church in North America. Early in 1942, he played a dominant role in the formation of the Federation for the Primary Jurisdiction of the Orthodox Greek Churches in America.

In March 1960, he spearheaded the reorganization of the Federation into the much stronger Standing Conference of Orthodox Bishops of the Americas (SCOBA). His leadership in these efforts for unity was best described by Fr Alexander Schmemann, dean of St Vladimir's Seminary:

[10]Salem, *Metropolitan Antony Bashir*, 19.

From the point of view of unity, he was truly the initiator, which cannot be said of many other people. He was truly independent. He was always a kind of spokesman for the Church. He would not take the rhetoric with which bishops were very often satisfied. They sit around the table and say "We are one," and they know very well we are not one.[11]

Metropolitan Antony wanted to move forward and create real unity. However, there was an ambiguous quality about SCOBA from its beginning. It was not de facto unity, but only the organ designed to bring about that unity. The other bishops were satisfied to meet once a year, eat lunch together, and discuss a few problems without ever taking the next step. Metropolitan Antony, however, was not. He knew actual unity would be difficult to achieve, but he also knew that it could never be achieved unless the different churches attempted it. He was fearless in his call for unity. As Fr Schmemann remarked: "Antony was always direct. He would say, 'Iakovos [Archbishop of the Greek Archdiocese], you know very well that this is not true. Don't cover that with flowery words. You know very well that we do not cooperate yet and that we should have done more.' "[12]

Even as he reaffirmed the preservation of the Orthodox faith and tradition, and despite the many imposing challenges and difficulties within the archdiocese and without, Antony continued to insist on jurisdictional unity. Wherever he traveled or served, he proclaimed the consistent message of unity.

Making Friends and Not Enemies

Metropolitan Antony believed that it was wiser to make friends than enemies. He distinguished himself as a notable leader in part by promoting closer friendship between the Orthodox Church and other religious groups. He was the first Orthodox bishop to join the National Council of Churches and was elected as the organization's vice-president in December 1960. He was also active in the World

[11]Schmemann, personal interview.
[12]Ibid.

Council of Churches and represented the Patriarchate at many international conferences. His relationship with non-Orthodox bodies earned him the worldwide respect of Catholic, Protestant, Jewish, and Muslim leaders alike.

A Footnote to History

Metropolitan Antony did not function in a vacuum. Nor did he issue edicts from on high, like some Greek god. The Antiochian Archdiocese is a community of parishes; it is a community of many people. A metropolitan is the leader to whom they look for guidance, vision, and inspiration. The issues grappled with by Metropolitan Antony were issues facing the archdiocese as a community, as a collective unit. Ultimately, it was up to the people of the archdiocese to embrace the cause of Christ in their lives and their churches, just as today the people of the archdiocese must embrace the future for themselves, their children, and their Church.

In the Antiochian Archdiocese, the collegiality of bishop, clergy, and people was expressed most clearly at the annual conventions. Here, the unity of leadership and laity, seeking together to further the cause of Christ for their generation and lay the foundations for that cause in the next, can be clearly seen. The report of the Sixth Convention, held in Indianapolis in August 1951, is of particular interest in this regard. It is, moreover, a witness to some of the great pastoral achievements of Metropolitan Antony. For these reasons, it is included below. For the sake of brevity, only the pertinent sections are given.

> The session was opened by Metropolitan Antony Bashir with a prayer. Archbishop Samuel David was present with clerical and lay delegates from the parishes of North America. Metropolitan Antony presided; Archbishop Samuel David served as vice-chairman of the convention.

> **Section II.** Metropolitan Antony reported the following:

A. SEMINARIANS

Our Archdiocese today, thanks to Almighty God, enjoys peace and harmony through the cooperation and Christian devotion and loyalty of the churches and parishes, plus the sincere efforts of his Eminence Archbishop Samuel David of Toledo. We have been working most harmoniously in attending to the spiritual needs of our parishioners in America.

The most important subject in our Archdiocese at the present time, as noted from the minutes of the previous convention and the Board of Trustees' report, is the education of the candidates for the holy priesthood.

We have been experiencing and studying various methods. Last year, as was arranged at the previous convention, we believed that our students should study with the Greek boys at the Greek Theological School in Brookline, Massachusetts. We tried that plan by sending three of our boys to this school. The boys did not like the school for the following reasons:

1. The school in Brookline is purely a Greek institution.

2. The students are required to learn Greek through and through, and become Greek in their spirit and their language.

Of course, handling a difficult problem like this requires lots of patience with the students, and lots of wisdom. We cannot force American boys to do anything against their will; therefore, we gave up this idea after careful thought and hard experience. We didn't lose much money because the officials of the Greek Seminary were very considerate and just charged a nominal fee. This will be reported in the financial report of the treasury.

Our next step was to attempt to establish a school of our own, by renting a house in Boston or Worcester, Massachusetts, as was suggested last year at the Cleveland convention. This idea was also studied thoroughly, and it proved impractical for the simple reason that the dignity of a graduate of any school is measured by the standing of the school itself. We were convinced, together with the Board of Trustees, that a school of our own for training clergymen is not feasible for the present.

Finally, we were obliged, by the hard facts of life, that the best alternative was to follow the Russian-American system of training candidates for holy orders by sending the candidate from high school or college to Columbia University in New York. There they get academic training and receive their degree from Columbia; studying at the same time at St Vladimir's Orthodox Seminary and Academy. This is affiliated by special arrangement with Columbia University. The religious courses that the students study at St Vladimir's Seminary are taught in English by the most eminent scholars of the Orthodox world.

The outstanding scholars in the Orthodox world who make up the faculty of St Vladimir's school are famous professors from colleges and universities in Eastern Europe who were driven away from their homes by the Communists and the Nazis, and finally settled in New York, and organized this Orthodox institution of learning. Because of their valuable training and important standing as scholars, Columbia University authorized them to teach Orthodox theology to students of our faith while studying at Columbia.

All religious courses taken at St Vladimir's are credited towards their degree. Under this system, the student will complete his B.A. degree from Columbia in three years instead of four, the usual term, because the extra religious courses are credited to the students at Columbia University. This saves the boy one year in college.

We were convinced beyond any doubt that this is the best system for us to utilize at the present time, and we are awaiting the happy day when our Patriarchate of Antioch will establish a good seminary in Beirut, Lebanon, where the students will be enrolled to graduate from the American university of Beirut, as well as the Orthodox Seminary.

We have for the present thirteen (13) Divinity students. Some of these boys are studying for the present at colleges and universities in their home towns, preparing themselves for Columbia and St Vladimir's; others are now at Columbia and St Vladimir's.

We are doing our best to augment their college education with study of the Arabic language, to enable them to use Arabic in their future services. Each of them is under the supervision of a spiritual preceptor to direct them in their studies and train them in the practical knowledge of performing their duties and divine services.

B. RELIGIOUS EDUCATION OF OUR YOUTH

For the religious education of our youth in the Sunday Schools, and at their homes, we have prepared and published various books. This literature is very essential to each church and home. We urge the reverend fathers, the church committees, and the parents in each Orthodox home to use them. The old as well as the young need the knowledge that these books impart.

Each book contains instructions to the teacher and the parent on how to teach each lesson. Each book contains forty lessons, in three sections: Bible Study, Church Study, and Doctrine & Faith.

Every lesson should be taught as outlined in the book. There is no excuse for any family or any priest for neglecting the duty of having these books and using them. The titles are as follows:

1. Beginners
2. Primary
3. Juniors
4. Intermediate
5. Advanced
6. Catechism of Christian Doctrine
7. Forty Saints
8. Orthodox Christian Year
9. Divine Liturgy
10. Pocket Prayer Book

These are essential to every Sunday school. Any criticism of the clergy for the lack of material for religious instruction is unjustified.

For Sunday school teachers, as well as our parishioners, we have prepared and published the following:

1. *Studies in the Greek Church*
   a. a brief history of the Orthodox Church;
   b. a detailed explanation of all rituals, symbols, and divine services;
   c. the doctrine and faith of the Orthodox Church.

2. *The Service Book*
   a. prayers for the Divine Service commonly used in church.

3. *The Priest's Guide*

    a. duties and rights of priest, church committees, and parishioners;

    b. planning the way for performing all services by priests in a uniform system to maintain the beauty and dignity of the church service.

C. CHURCH CHOIRS

For the choir of our churches, we have prepared and published two beautiful books called: (1) *Orthodox Hymns in English*, and (2) *Three Divine Liturgies and Other Prayers with Music* (two of these liturgies are in Arabic pronunciation with the words spelled in phonetic English). To produce good results in the use of these books, every church must have a choir. A church without a choir is like a body without a soul.

The church committee of every parish must realize that the little money they spend for a musical director to organize a choir is the best investment possible for the progress of their congregation. They should insist on the cooperation of their priest and spare no money and effort to organize and conduct a choir and Sunday school.

D. THE CLERGY

During the last convention it was decided that the priests should be authorized to call on organizations and individuals for contributions to the treasury of the Archdiocese. The priests who did make these calls were very successful in aiding the Archdiocese fund.

Our success as an organization depends principally on the clergy as, with all due respect to the laymen, they are too busy with their own activities, which permit them very little time to devote to church problems. Therefore, I suggested at this convention to give the clergy more and more authority and responsibility. Hold the priest responsible and give him enough authority, and I assure you that there is no priest who will not be able to produce good results.

People respect the priest and do not turn him down when he calls for a worthy cause. We need the help of the priests in organizing good choirs and Sunday schools, and in backing the church committees in their local parishes.

Unfortunately we have lost several of our older priests during the last year. Several churches in the Archdiocese are closed. We have not been able to find the proper candidates worthy for the priesthood for immediate ordination. Regretfully, some of those churches must remain closed until our boys graduate. This year three of them will be ready for ordination.

The above report by Metropolitan Antony was unanimously accepted, with sincere thanks for his great efforts.

[Sections III–X omitted.]

Section XI.

The question of an Orthodox chaplain in the United States Armed Services, together with the proper recognition of our religion on the identification tag given to the servicemen, was opened for discussion.

His Eminence Metropolitan Antony, explained that as the president of the Federated Orthodox Greek Catholic Jurisdictions in America, and in behalf of all Orthodox bishops, he made several trips to Washington, where he took the matter up with the proper authorities of the United States government. The results of his work were as follows:

The government will welcome any Orthodox priest for service as a chaplain in the Armed Forces provided he meets their necessary qualifications. Those requirements are that he be between the ages of 23 to 33, and a graduate from an accredited American college and seminary.

There are very few priests at the present time who are able to satisfy these requirements, and those who do qualify are badly needed in their parishes. In time, we will have an ample number of qualified priests for this service, and the government will be glad to accept them as chaplains in the [armed] services.

Regarding the identification of the servicemen, His Eminence explained that during the last war the government, at his suggestion, printed on the identification tag the letter "O" to identify the servicemen of the Orthodox Faith.

When the services started to mark blood types on identification tags, it was found necessary to cancel this in view of the possibility of conflict with Type O blood. The letter "O" represents a certain blood type. This caused many doctors to be confused in urgent cases by quickly glancing at the tag, and mistaking the letter "O" for the type of blood instead of the religious faith. That was the principal reason for the discontinuation of the use of the letter "O" for the Orthodox boys. At the present time, they are using the letter "X."

[Sections XII–XV omitted.]

Section XVI.

It was recommended that a bulletin or a magazine should be sent periodically from the Archdiocese to the various parishes. Metropolitan Antony was authorized immediately to take the necessary measures for the issuing of such a periodical. [From the 1951 Convention to the present a complimentary copy of *The Word* magazine has been sent to all the families of the archdiocese.]

CHAPTER 10

A Most Untimely
and Unexpected Death

*We shall follow you, and we shall ever fight for the principles
which you have lived and died for. And let Satan, the master of
deceit and dissension, know that we are more united than ever,
and that in each and everyone of us there is a spark from the eternal torch which Antony Bashir has carried throughout his entire
life.[1]*

T he death of Metropolitan Antony marked the end of an important era in the history of the American Orthodox Church in
general, and of the Antiochian Church in particular. During his
thirty years of spiritual leadership as metropolitan, Antony had been
directly responsible for the Archdiocese's tremendous growth and
achievements. When he departed to his heavenly Father, he left behind
him an archdiocese that was well organized on every level: physically,
with regions and deaneries; spiritually, with an educated clergy serving healthy local parishes; and financially, built upon a strong foundation of frugality.

The Final Illness Begins

In November 1965, Metropolitan Antony underwent treatment at the
New York Memorial Hospital for a disease of the lymphatic system.
In spite of his failing health, however, he continued to fulfill his spiri-

---

[1]Metropolitan Philip (Saliba), in *The Word* 10. 4–5 (April-May 1966): 4.

tual duties. He was able to celebrate the Divine Liturgy at St Mary's Church in Brooklyn on January 30, 1966; it was to be his last public service. On February 7, "he felt so uncomfortable that he decided to seek additional treatment in Boston. He flew there on the following day accompanied by Fr Paul Schneirla."[2]

Fr George R. George, the pastor of St George Church in Boston, along with Monsour Laham, met them at Logan Airport. Fr George recalls:

> We immediately took him to Lancy Clinic where, after a lengthy exam, he was admitted to the New England Baptist Hospital on Parker Hill Road in Boston. The prognosis of his affliction was not good . . . The doctors said that he had melanoma, which is akin to leukemia. He was allowed to rest for the remainder of that day and the following day, after which he was taken to MIT for the first of a series of treatments with the cobalt machine, one of only two in this country.[3]

Metropolitan Antony's sister Adele, brother Saba, and nephew Tony, plus Fr George and his wife, Fr Paul Moses, and several members of the Archdiocesan Board of Trustees, were near him night and day, praying for his recovery. "The late Cardinal Cushing visited him . . . and this seemed to cheer him up. He always had an extreme softness in his heart for Cardinal Cushing."[4]

On Tuesday morning, February 15, he received the sacraments from Fr George. A rumor later developed that Cardinal Cushing, during his visit, had administered the sacraments to Metropolitan Antony, but Fr George offered this categorical denial:

> One thing I would like to clear up here . . . for the rumor seems to persist: Cardinal Cushing *did not*, I repeat, *did not* give him the sacrament of communion . . . It was I myself who administered holy oil and the sacrament of penance and communion to him on

[2]*The Word* 10. 3 (March 1966): 4.
[3]From a personal letter of Rev. George R. George, sent to the author, and dated May 8, 1972.
[4]Ibid.

his request and the request of his sister Adele. This act shall forever be a part of me.[5]

And the End Came Quickly

Metropolitan Antony knew he was terminally ill, but thought he had "at least two more years to live."[6] Adele was astonished to hear her brother asking her why she had come to see him. "You should have stayed at the Archdiocese headquarters," he said, "you cannot help me here. I will be all right. The doctors told me I will be cured."[7] However, on February 16, 1966, one day after receiving holy communion, Metropolitan Antony departed to eternity. The news of his death spread quickly across the Archdiocese. His passing away, only one short week after his arrival in Boston, was a shock to everyone, and his death was deeply felt in the hearts of those who knew him and had served with him.[8]

Metropolitan Antony's body lay in state at St Nicholas Cathedral in Brooklyn from Friday, February 18, until the funeral on Wednesday, February 23. During that time, the cathedral was visited by thousands of mourners, and prayer services for his repose were conducted by hierarchs, clergy, and choirs representing every Orthodox jurisdiction in the United States.[9]

On a personal note, my father was serving as a priest in Danbury, Connecticut, when news came that Metropolitan Antony had passed away. He went to New York, and I went with him. When we arrived, the metropolitan was laid out in St Nicholas Cathedral. Clergy and laity from the Archdiocese were there along with the patriarchal representative, Metropolitan Ilyas Kurban.

I later saw Archbishop Michael Shaheen arrive with his entourage. Raphael Husson was with him, as were Mary and Anna Douad and others. I knew, of course, about the tensions between the Archdiocese

---

[5]Ibid.
[6]Ibid.
[7]Adele Khoury, personal interview.
[8]Rev. George R. George, personal letter.
[9]*The Word* 10. 3 (March 1966): 4.

and Toledo. Nonetheless I was stunned to see that, with the sole exception of Metropolitan Ilyas Kurban, no clergy were present in the cathedral when Archbishop Michael arrived. Instead, our clergy were gathered in the basement with the protosyngellos, Fr Elias Khoury, discussing the future of the Archdiocese and the steps to be taken to elect a new metropolitan. Archbishop Michael conducted a trisagion service and then departed with his entourage.

The Funeral Service

The cathedral was packed for the funeral. There were Orthodox as well as non-Orthodox bishops from across the country. One kept hearing such comments as "great loss," "he left a vacuum," "too young," "what a gifted speaker," "he was stern in spirit." Emotions ran high. The funeral service began with the Liturgy of the Presanctified Gifts, celebrated by the dean of St Vladimir's Seminary, Fr Alexander Schmemann, and sung by the seminary choir. The funeral itself was led by the patriarchal representative, Metropolitan Ilyas Kurban of Tripoli. Many other hierarchs served with him. Metropolitan Ilyas delivered the following eulogy:

> *I am the good shepherd; the good shepherd giveth his life for the sheep. I am the good shepherd and know my sheep, and am known of mine.* (John 14:10, 14)

There are no more fitting words to be said in such a painful chapter. We are gathering together from every part of this large continent and from abroad to bid farewell to the good shepherd. This good shepherd holds in the hearts of us all that note of love, of deep respect, of appreciation, and of affection. No eulogy and no words can describe nor enumerate the great achievements of our beloved departed metropolitan. Yet, if we do not speak, the stones must open their mouths. If we remain silent, the days of this great man must narrate his great deeds and his great works.

One man has accomplished in his lifetime what many communities failed in the annals of history. His dynamism and his vitality were incomparable. The history of his life becomes a legend,

PHOTOGRAPHIC ARCHIVES

Toronto Convention 1964. Some of the clergy and archdiocese trustees.

Right: Metropolitan Antony and Pope Paul. October 1964.

Below:
At St Valdimir's Seminary (seated L to R): Metropolitan Andrey— Bulgarian Church, Metropolitan Antony, Metropolitan Leonty, Archbishop Germanos of Nyssa (representing Archbishop Iakavos of the Greek Archdiocese), (standing L to R): Archbishop John of Chicago, Archbishop John of San Francisco, Arcbishop Ireney of Boston, and Bishop Kiprian of Washington & all of the Russian Orthodox Church. March 1963.

Metropolitan Antony & Bishop Fulton J. Sheen, Auxiliary Bishop of the Catholic Archdiocese of New York, at the SOYO Convention. September 1962.

Patriarch Theodosios, Metropolitan Antony and Monsour Laham. January 1959.

A poignant moment on Metropolitan Antony's Boston trip comes on a visit to a retired priest and old friend, the Rt. Rev. Abdullah Shaker. January 1963.

Metropolitan Antony at his desk in Brooklyn, NY, 1962.

Metropolitan Antony with a life-long friend, Patriarch Athenagoras. March 1966.

*Metropolitan Antony
giving the blessing
the end of his last
Archdiocesan
Convention in
August 1965.*

Syrian Antiochian Archdiocese Tour. January 1959.

Metropolitan Antony with his family in Mexico. His mother is seated in the black dress. His two sisters, Adele and Najla, are also shown.

Metropolitan Antony with his niece Linda Kasin Brown.

Metropolitan Antony Bashir.

Metropolitan Antony with his elder brother Saba Bashir.

Metropolitan Antony with his cousin Gabriel Ayoub (L) and his brother Saba Bashir (R).

Metropolitan Antony blessing the Bashir Auditorium at St Vladimir's Seminary. Archbishop Iakavos on the left. Fr Alexander Schmemann on the far left.

and Metropolitan Antony is now numbered among the great hierarchs of the Holy Church. His legacy to the Archdiocese of New York and all North America, to the see of Antioch, and to the Universal Church is measureless. His contribution to the literary movement in the Middle East, in all the Arab lands, and the Americas, is great.

Over one hundred churches, religious centers, and schools were erected during his pastorship. He was one of the first Orthodox hierarchs who introduced English in the divine service of the Church in North America. It was he who sponsored the projects of religious education for children and adults. Over twenty-five religious books were published, and they are now in use. He watered and revitalized Orthodoxy. Orthodoxy is an active factor in the American society and a fact of American life. He has not "Americanized" the Church; rather, it is that he has made Orthodoxy a fact in America.

His service to the mother church has been a prompt reply to all the pleas and appeals for cultural, charitable, and building projects. It is a known fact that there is not a single Orthodox church in Lebanon and Syria that does not have some bibles or prayer books sent to her from the archbishop. He was a prominent factor in the organization of the Standing Conference of Orthodox Bishops in America.

The ecumenical movement was such an important chapter in his life. He represented the patriarch and the see of Antioch to the World Conference on Faith and Order at Oxford, England in 1938. The World Council of Churches was surely his interest. The call from Rome for unity increased his great favor and desire. His recent visit with Pope Paul of Rome was his further desire in love. The echo of his voice is yet heard on many campuses and in many churches of this nation. It would be impossible to enumerate all his deeds and achievements; yet, we cannot pass without mentioning that our beloved departed metropolitan has pledged finally to build the Balamand Theological School. It will overlook the blue Mediterranean sea from one side, and the eternal cedars of Lebanon from the other. This theological school will be a great monument to this great archbishop, as a tribute to his life for years to come. The fruitful life of the great shepherd has come to an end. He fell as a courageous soldier. He has left in this shepherding of the sheep the faith, the devotion, and the dedication he best knew how to give.

Listen, and we can hear him [speaking] in the words of the Apostle Paul: "I have fought a good fight, I have finished my course, I have kept the faith." (II Tim. 4:7) The close bond with the departed and beloved metropolitan has caused His Beatitude Patriarch Theodosius of the see of Antioch and the Holy Synod to send me to be with you at this sad and painful time. In his name, in their name, and in mine, I convey to the family, the clergy, the Board of Trustees, and the flock of the Archdiocese of New York and all North America our most sincere sympathy and condolences. In behalf of His Beatitude the Patriarch and the Synod of Antioch with her clergy, my most humble gratitude to the primate, my brother in Christ, Archbishop Iakovos of the Greek Orthodox Church in America, as the representative of His Holiness the Ecumenical Patriarch Athenagoras, for his presence and his kind words. Our most humble gratitude to all who are present, primates and representatives of sister Orthodox churches, of all other Christian bodies, and of the civil and diplomatic authorities and dignitaries.

With the Saints give rest to thy departed servant where there is no sickness, nor sorrow, nor sighing, but life everlasting.[10]

We Shall Follow You

Fr Philip Saliba was chosen to deliver the eulogy on behalf of the clergy of the archdiocese who had served under Metropolitan Antony:

If our beloved Metropolitan Antony were to give his spiritual children a farewell address, I am sure that he would have said what St Paul did say to the Corinthians: "Ye brethren: I beseech you, by

[10]Ilyas Kurban, 'Sermon at the Funeral of Metropolitan Antony,' *The Word* 10. 4–5 (April-May 1966): 5.

the name of Our Lord Jesus Christ, that ye all speak the same thing, and that there be no divisions among you; but that ye be perfectly joined together in the same mind and in the same judgment" (I Corinthians 1:10).

No eulogy, no speech, and no lecture is sufficient to describe the greatness of this prince of the Church. When, in the future, historians will write the history of the Orthodox in America, the name of Metropolitan Antony Bashir will shine like the stars of heaven.

The motto of his entire life was these divine words recorded in the Gospel of St. John: "My Father works, and I work also" (St. John 5:17). What he has accomplished in his fifty years cannot be achieved in two hundred years. Metropolitan Antony was not a picture on the wall, he was very much alive and he will continue to live in the memory of the Church forever.

One of his most cherished dreams was to educate an army of dedicated clergy for the ministry of the gospel. We thank God that his dream was realized before he departed this life to life eternal. To us, the clergy of this strong archdiocese, he was not an archbishop only; he was a friend and a father. St Paul said, "for though ye have ten thousand instructors in Christ, yet ye have not many fathers, for in Christ Jesus I have begotten you through the gospel. Wherefore I beseech you, be ye followers of me" (I Corinthians 4:15–16).

Yes, your Eminence, we shall follow you, and we shall ever fight for the principles which you have lived and died for. And let Satan, the master of deceit and dissension, know that we are more united than ever, and that in each and everyone of us there is a spark from the eternal torch which Antony Bashir has carried throughout his entire life.[11]

---

[11]Fr Philip Saliba, 'We Shall Follow You,' *The Word* 10. 4–5 (April-May 1966): 4.

The Collective Memory of a Community

No man can ever take fully the measure of another. Even were it possible to know perfectly another man's heart, it would be a knowledge nevertheless ineffable, impossible to express in words. In this life "we know in part"; it is only in the life to come that we shall know fully and be fully known.[12] Yet while each person forever remains a mystery, in the collective memory of a community many of the pieces of the puzzle can be put together, allowing a clearer picture of the man to emerge. In addition to the eulogies of Metropolitan Ilyas and Fr Philip, the three following eulogies help us to appreciate better the life and legacy of Metropolitan Antony. The first was delivered by Archbishop Iakovos of the Greek Archdiocese of North and South America.

> It was early morning in Athens last Thursday, when I received the most unexpected and shocking news that my respected and beloved fellow servant in the vineyard of American Orthodoxy, Metropolitan Antony Bashir, "entered through the gates into the City of God" (Revelation 22:14).
>
> Another city, the violet-crowned city, the sacred city of the ancient Hellenes, Athens, was at that very moment rising from slumber and awakening to the glorious morning, marking the beginning of a new day. I stood for a moment both grieved and speechless, and I offered a prayer to Him who is the Resurrection, the Life Itself.
>
> In the reflection of that clear, diamond-studded blue morning sky, I thought for a moment that I saw my friend, stately, dignified, smiling happily as he always did, and ascending, together with the sun, majestically towards the gates of heaven, singing, Alleluia! His whole life was an alleluia, for he lived for the glory of God.
>
> His was a ministry inspired and guided by the love of his flock, by his faith in God, and by his vision of a united Orthodox Church in the American continent. Studious, courageous, and richly

[12]1 Corinthians 13.9, 12.

gifted, he pioneered the way towards the modern interpretation of the ancient Church of the East to the new worlds of the West.

He personally labored for long years to make available the spiritual treasures of Orthodoxy to all, by devoting much of his time translating, editing, and publishing the most important of our liturgical rites and offices. He was a great enthusiast of theological education and a generous supporter of Orthodox theological institutions. The theological school at Balamand, over Tripoli in Lebanon, and St Vladimir's Theological Seminary, owe much of their present modern establishments and facilities to the benevolence of Antony Bashir.

In addition, he enabled many worthy students to pursue a theological education at Holy Cross as well as St Vladimir's and thus qualify themselves for the ministration of the spiritual needs of the Syrian Antiochian faithful. A number of the young priests mourn today not only their spiritual leader, but their personal benefactor as well.

He was the first ever to introduce English into our liturgical practices, and prepared the first Sunday school books in English, for he foresaw the needs of the Church, which would someday be serving American-born and educated generations of Orthodox Christians.

Antony Bashir, being himself an enlightened man, fought all his life for what he called a period of Christian enlightenment that would abolish once and for all the darkness of doubt and fear and illuminate and terminate the blindness of religious ignorance and of church-sponsored bias and prejudiced practices.

Determined as he was, he broke away from the Orthodox custom which was to react always with suspicion, and he received into the rank of his clergy—through ordination—ministers and priests of other Christian faiths who would, by their own volition, express their wish to serve him and his Orthodox flock.

He advocated the cause of the reunion of the Church even before the World Council of Churches or the National Council of Churches or the Vatican Council came into being. As an Orthodox theologian and clergyman, offspring of the ever-suffering and praying Christian East, he would not yield to any pressure.

He understood his ministry in terms of promoting understanding, charity, and hope among all Christians. Antony Bashir, being gifted with an extraordinary positive and practical mind, believed that inter-church or ecumenical relations could not be built unless the Orthodox would unite among themselves and jointly act and project and promote ecumenical mindedness. It was for this reason that twenty-four years ago, in the month of March of 1942, together with my great predecessor, Athenagoras, the present Ecumenical Patriarch, he initiated the first movement of uniting the Orthodox of the United States into one unit, into one jurisdiction, into one American Orthodox Church.

It was for this very same reason that Antony Bashir, together with the late Metropolitan Leonty, responded to my request that we reanimate and reactivate the desire for a united Orthodox Church in the Western hemisphere. His was a role of architect as well as mediator and peacemaker, and, as long as the Standing Conference of Canonical Orthodox Bishops stands, we shall thank God for giving us Antony Bashir.

Acting in behalf of the Orthodox hierarchs, I offer you, the spiritual children, clergy and lay people of the Syrian Antiochian Church, our personal warmest condolences, as well as the sincere and wholehearted expression of sympathy of our constituencies, and pray together with you for the repose of the noble soul of your gallant arch-soldier and leader.

To the most reverend and eminent representative of the highly honored and revered great Patriarch of Antioch and of all East, may I offer the assurance of our brotherly compassion and solidarity at this moment of mourning and grief, and of our prayers that God, through your synod, may bless the American Syrian Orthodox Church with a man of the same Orthodox conviction, insight, and prophetic mind that Antony Bashir personified.

And to all, Orthodox and non-Orthodox Christians alike, who mourn the untimely death and grievous loss of a churchman, who was an assurance and a promise of the divine things to come

- 6

into our reawakened Christian consciences and lives, and who furthermore, and foremost, was your friend and brother and father and leader, may I offer an exhortation on behalf of your archbishop's great friend, Patriarch Athenagoras: "If we believe that Jesus died and rose again, even so them also which sleep in Jesus will God bring with Him . . . Wherefore comfort yourselves together and edify one another so that whether we wake or sleep we should live together with Christ" (I Thessalonians 4:14; 5:10–11).[13]

The second eulogy was delivered by Monsour H. Laham in his capacity as the lay chairman of the Archdiocese Board of Trustees.

The passing of our Metropolitan Antony marks the end of a most important era in the history of the Orthodox Church in America. It was a time of tremendous growth and achievement, and he was responsible for much of it. He was our bishop and leader for thirty years, a whole generation, and he set his stamp on everything and everybody he had to do with during that time.

For the first ten years of this time, he *was* the Archdiocese solely and singly. Some twenty years ago it became apparent that the time had come for help, and so the present system of organization of our Archdiocese was drafted, and we of the Archdiocesan Board of Trustees were privileged to help in his great work.

The last twenty years have seen the gradual fruition of his efforts, and we are proud to have been a part of this man's life work. He was the friend and associate of many of the world's great men, and to us he also was a great man. Like all great men, he learned from everyone, and he taught everyone. There is not one of us who has not benefited from his wisdom and profited by his inspiration.

Always under pressure, he was unsparing of his patience and ready with his understanding. He was always ready to listen to the ideas of those with whom he had to work. It is hard for us who stood so close to him in affection and endeavor to assess correctly

[13]Archbishop Iakovos, *The Word* 10. 3 (March 1966): 5–6.

the magnitude of the work that he did, but this will be the task of those who come after. But we all know that by him the foundations of the future of the Syrian Antiochian Orthodox Church were laid, and that whatever the future brings forth will be built on those foundations.

As our chief pastor, he was a true Father in God. He was concerned about us and with us; he knew us all by name, and he was concerned closely with our problems. He traveled hundreds of thousands of miles over this continent, up and down, back and forth; and all for the benefit of individuals of his flock. In the first decade of his mission, he practically lived and worked on board railroad trains; he wrote thousands of letters in Arabic and English by hand as he went. In the thirties people did not fly as they do now, and in one year he traveled more than 65,000 miles by train, in addition to automobile and other journeys. When it became possible to fly, he flew; not because it made things easier, but because he could get more done.

He had enormous energy and capacity for work. He made others work and achieve more than they ever knew they could. He is gone, but a part of him remains with each of us with whom and for whom he worked. We shall not forget him; we are his living monument, for he helped to make so many of us what we are. With all the others not of his flock who were influenced by him, we recognize that here was a great man, and in the deepest knowledge of this we pay him our most sincere tribute: for he loved us, and we loved him.[14]

The third eulogy reproduced here came from John Khoury, chancellor of the Antiochian Archdiocese.

By his deeds shall ye know him . . .
Institutions do not make men, men make institutions.

As we address our Metropolitan tonight to permit him to take with him a message to greener vineyards, to a better life, free of pain and suffering, free of anguish, free of tension, and free of

[14]Ibid., 6–7.

pressure, we can only do what all of us are doing, and that is to take a bit of historic inventory of what this man has been to this institution—the American Orthodox Church, and its smallest branch, the Syrian Orthodox Church.

If we were to address you, Saidna, with this message, and if we were humbly to take the chance that we paraphrase some of the holy words and if we, in my generation, to whom you came thirty years ago representing the tomb which is the transition and the challenge that you faced, we might say that you came to us when we were hungry in the faith, and you fed us; you came to us when we were naked of organization, and you clothed us; you came to us when we were imprisoned by confusion, and you stabilized us; you came to us when we were thirsty for leadership, and you gave it to us to drink of your wisdom. You came to us when the bloodstream of the church was anemic, and you nourished it with the iron of a strong will.

And if I were to read your spiritual will to us, I would paraphrase it like this: I, Antony Bashir, Metropolitan, realizing the uncertainty of this too short life that you live, do hereby declare this to be my last spiritual will and testament; I give to you an efficient and well-organized archdiocese; I give to you a well-established and continuous educational program; I give you a well-qualified clergy; I give to you an ecumenical spirit of wholesome realization with people of all faiths; I give you SOYO, my movement, and I implore you as I leave to intercede for you, to continue that which my humble efforts began.

Depart, faithful servant; may your memory be eternal.[15]

Messages of Sympathy

The archdiocese office received thousands of tributes and messages of sympathy at the time of Metropolitan Antony's death. They were received from hierarchs of the Orthodox Church, civil authorities, representatives of religious societies, leaders of other Christian bod-

[15]Ibid., 7.

ies, and from public figures. The broad response to the passing of Metropolitan Antony testified to the stature he had attained personally, but more importantly, it testified to the public visibility that the Orthodox Church in America had attained in large part because of this man. His death did not go unnoticed, for the Orthodox Church no longer went unnoticed. This was true even at the highest levels, as the follow telegrams and messages indicate:

> Deeply sorry on the passing of our beloved Metropolitan Antony. We pray God rest his soul. We express to you all our cordial sympathy. Our Archdiocese will represent us at the funeral service.
>
> ### PATRIARCH ATHENAGORAS
> Archbishop of Constantinople,
> New Rome, and Ecumenical Patriarch[16]

> Paternal condolences. We pray the Lord rests his soul in peace and encourage his spiritual flock.
>
> ### PATRIARCH BENEDICTOS
> Patriarch of Jerusalem[17]

> In sorrow our holy Church prays for the departed spirit of Metropolitan Antony.
>
> ### PATRIARCH ALEXI
> Patriarch of Moscow and all Russia[18]

> The death of Metropolitan Antony Bashir brings sadness not only to the hearts of the members of his Syrian Antiochian Orthodox Church, but to all who cherish human freedom and righteousness. His life was rich in service to God and to his fellow man. His enduring contributions were many and great. I join with sorrow those who mourn his passing, and I express to each of you my personal sympathy at his loss.
>
> ### LYNDON B. JOHNSON
> President of the United States[19]

[16]Ibid., 8.
[17]Ibid.
[18]Ibid.
[19]Ibid., 9–10.

I am very sorry indeed to learn of the death of the Most Reverend Metropolitan Archbishop Antony Bashir and extend deepest condolences to you and the faithful of your church.

L. B. PEARSON
Prime Minister of Canada[20]

With deep sorrow and grief I learn of the passing away of our beloved Metropolitan Antony Bashir. His death is most untimely and unexpected. His work at building the Orthodox Church of the Patriarchate of Antioch in the United States of America is a living example of his leadership and accomplishment. He shall be missed for the many great things he has lived and strived for. Deepest condolences to you and to all the parishioners in the Archdiocese of North America.

SOUHEIL CHAMMAS
Charge D' Affaires,
Permanent Mission of Lebanon
to the United States[21]

Learned with deep sorrow the untimely passing away of His Eminence Metropolitan Antony Bashir, head of the Syrian Antiochian Orthodox Church of North America. He will be remembered always for his progressive work, his spiritual guidance, and the great service he rendered to Lebanon and his fellow countrymen of all faiths. On behalf of the Ambassador El-Ahdab and the entire staff of the Embassy of Lebanon in Washington, we extend to you and to your entire community our sincerest condolences.

KHALIL MAKKAWI
Charge D' Affaires *ad interim*
of Lebanon (Washington, DC)[22]

Those of us who were privileged to feel the touch of the strong, helpful hands of our beloved Metropolitan Antony and to hear the wisdom of his teachings and experience the joy of his most com-

[20]Ibid., 10.
[21]Ibid.
[22]Ibid., 11.

forting smile have suffered the loss of a priceless treasure on earth, but have gained a new intercessor in Heaven. May he pray for us.

DANNY THOMAS
Actor and Philanthropist
Los Angeles, California [23]

[23]Ibid., 13.

PART II

Personal Remembrances of Metropolitan Antony

CHAPTER 11

Casting a Long Shadow

O n the eve of his funeral, as Antony Bashir lay in state, a multitude of prelates in black robes filed in and began to chant in a multitude of languages. Observing these prelates, the late Protosyngellos Ellis Khouri commented quietly, "In his death he still looms larger than most of these gentlemen do in life!"[1]

Heartfelt grief, especially the grief caused by an untimely and totally unexpected death, can be forgiven if it resorts to hyperbole to express the enormity of the loss. With the passing of time, however, the wounds of grief heal and a clearer assessment of the life of a man can be given. Some historians believe that a minimum of fifty years must pass before an accurate history of events or people can be composed—for to the eyewitnesses it is not yet history, but still memory.

Over Forty Years Later

At the time of this writing, it has been just over forty years since the passing of Antony Bashir. Although we have not yet reached the fifty-year threshold, enough time has passed to begin an objective assessment of the life and accomplishments of Antony Bashir. The question is not how tall he stood in comparison to his contemporaries, but how tall he stands when judged by history. How long a shadow does his life cast?

Ultimately, history must judge the length of Bashir's shadow within the context of both the Antiochian Archdiocese and the larger

[1]Protosyngellos Ellis Khouri, cited in Antony Gabriel, 'Lest We Forget: The Administrative Legacy of Antony Bashir (1936–1966),' (unpublished article, Montreal, Canada: July, 1997), 2.

history of the American Orthodox Church. But another measure of his shadow's length can be found in the lives of those who knew him and who have outlived him. We may ask just how long a shadow he has cast in their lives as the years have gone by.

Six years after Bashir's death, Monsour H. Laham—who as the lay chairman of the Antiochian Archdiocesan board had witnessed many of the private meetings between members of the Toledo group, Samuel David, Michael Shaheen, and Metropolitan Antony—said that one of the many reasons he consistently supported Bashir was because of Bashir's conduct throughout. Watching Bashir under attack had given Laham an insight into Bashir's character, into what "made him tick," as it were. He once observed:

> I know that no human being is an angel; none of us is perfect. But I learned back in the 1940s that Antony Bashir's only interest was the welfare of the Church and nothing else. That was so obvious from the way he worked and slaved just to establish the well-being of the Church, particularly in this country. He had a very high regard for the mother church in spite of the heartbreaks it caused him. The man was a man of God, and the welfare of the Church was uppermost in his mind. His own person meant nothing to him. This is my judgment of him. What he accomplished was of great importance; he thought nothing of his personal convenience. The man never asked for himself, only for the Church and for others who were in need. He asked those who could afford it to help the Church and others. He was like a prophet, way ahead of his time. Men like that don't come around every day. Unfortunately, he did not live to see the fruits of his accomplishments. He was well respected by all in the Church, by other denominations, and even by the government that had grown to know him. The Archdiocese had money to fund Balamand because of the sacrifice of Antony Bashir. Balamand was one of his dreams.[2]

---

[2]Monsour Laham, personal interview.

Fr Alexander Schmemann: An Independent Assessment

Fr Alexander Schmemann was a Russian-born priest who served the Orthodox Church in America. Coming from outside the Antiochian Archdiocese, he perceived Antony Bashir from a different, and perhaps more independent, perspective. Schmemann's association with Bashir began when Antiochian students first started to attend St Vladimir's Seminary, where Schmemann was dean.

> I arrived in this country in 1951, and I'm sure that I met him then, because Fr Paul Schneirla was already teaching at St Vladimir's. However, we didn't have Antiochian students at first; they went to Holy Cross, the Greek seminary in Brookline. I think that the first Antiochian students were sent to the seminary in 1955. Our regular cooperation began when he decided that all his boys would no longer go to the Greek seminary but to our seminary, St Vladimir's.[3]

Antony Bashir was committed to building an Orthodox Church in North America. He did not accept the view that the immigrant church existed in a kind of diaspora, as a church in exile waiting to return to "the old country." Neither did he see the Church as a colony or outpost of "the old country." Prior to the 1950s, this "old country" mentality still shaped both Holy Cross and St Vladimir's seminaries. When things began to change at St Vladimir's, however, Antony acted quickly. According to Fr. Schmemann,

> He immediately recognized that the team that organized St Vladimir's, or at least took over in the early fifties, was the nucleus of an American Orthodox reality. This is exactly what he had always said openly—that for him, St Vladimir's was not a Russian Seminary. He never used the term "Russian Seminary" when referring to St Vladimir's; he was always clear about it.[4]

[3]Schmemann, personal interview.
[4]Ibid.

Missed Opportunities: Education

Antony Bashir took pride in his frugality. What human weaknesses he had often became visible as a result of his deep-seated desire to pinch pennies. His miserly impulses often short-circuited the achievement of his larger goals—such as bringing an American Orthodox Church into existence—as he missed opportunities that could have furthered these goals. Two examples of this paradox, wherein his personal need for frugality sabotaged his ecclesiastical goals, can be seen in the matter of church education and in the Standing Conference of the Canonical Orthodox Bishops (SCOBA).

Antony Bashir believed, of course, in having an educated clergy. He endorsed St Vladimir's Seminary by sending Antiochian seminarians there, but as the saying goes, he did not put his money where his mouth is. Had he seized the opportunity to make a sizable infusion of funds, he could have realized his dream of an American Orthodox Seminary. Fr Schmemann offered these comments on Bashir's parsimony:

> Well, as you know, finances were another story with the metropolitan. He didn't want to disburse too much. I would say this: that he always paid his bills without any problems for his students, and that is already something. But we always had to fight with him, and we very often fought to increase his support for the seminary.
>
> Maybe it was something of his background, of that of many immigrants who come here more or less poor. Having made some money, they are extremely nervous about disbursing it. In that respect he was not very American, I would say. Americans like the deficit spending, going into mortgages and so on, but he still reflected that generation of people who lived in America through the Depression, for whom to give money was a very painful process.
>
> He supported St Vladimir's. I think that he supported it morally more than financially. He never opposed our financial efforts in his archdiocese. He never made any obstacles to them. But I think he could have done more financially, and his priorities . . . well, it doesn't concern only the seminary; it's like his head-

quarters, which were run at a minimum, with no staff, nothing. He just didn't want to pay anyone.[5]

Antony Bashir pinched pennies in order to finance Balamand in Lebanon, so that there would be an educated clergy in the Patriarchate of Antioch. However, although he sent his American students to St Vladimir's, he missed an opportunity not only to help finance St Vladimir's but also to place, once and for all, the need for Orthodox education firmly in the consciousness of the Church in America. Again, Fr Schmemann noted:

> I think that the churches in general and the Antiochian Church in particular all have a wrong sense of priorities. In fact, the Orthodox Church in this country could have really created a first-class, endowed institution; more than a seminary, an Orthodox university. All this would have been absolutely possible if people had not been tied to the idea that education is something additional. And I detect that same mentality still. Education always comes last; everything else comes first. Here I would be bitterly critical of the Church. Although I think that, since Metropolitan Antony's leadership, it's taken for granted that the Archdiocese has to help the seminary, I think that that help is still out of proportion to the real needs.[6]

Almost every religious body in the United States has at least one university. Some have one or more in several states, but there is no Orthodox university. There are private grade schools and upper schools sponsored by local churches all across the United States, but there are almost no Orthodox schools. The religious landscape is filled with churches with massive education wings for religious education on Sundays and other times throughout the week. Most Orthodox parishes, however, provide only a few small rooms for religious education, almost as an afterthought.

Had Antony Bashir made Christian education a major priority by leading the challenge to underwrite Christian education in America when he had the opportunity to do so, beginning in 1955, then the

[5]Ibid.
[6]Ibid.

state of religious education in the Orthodox Church in America today would be far different than it is. His personal need to hoard money caused him to miss this opportunity.

Missed Opportunities: SCOBA

A second opportunity was missed with the Standing Conference of the Canonical Orthodox Bishops in the Americas. Antony Bashir had a vision of a united church in America, an American Orthodox Church. On account of that vision, he became instrumental in forming SCOBA. He also possessed a real strength of leadership. He was a charismatic leader with an appealing, forceful personality. Fr Schmemann observed:

> He was very blunt and direct. He had very little use for theology as such. He was principally an administrator. He had a direct way of thinking and liked to go to the heart of the matter. He did not like the gradual approach to addressing an issue. In this he was not quite Oriental, but rather much more like an American businessman, in many respects. He was much too blunt and direct for the Middle Eastern ways. He simplified everything and even worked without a secretary most of the time.
>
> Metropolitan Antony was truly independent, and this cannot be said of many other people . . . [He] was always a kind of spokesman of truth. He wouldn't take the rhetoric with which bishops were very often satisfied. They sit around the table and say, "We are one," and they know very well that they are not one. There was a kind of ambiguity in the Standing Conference from the very beginning, because the Standing Conference was not the expression of unity, but rather the organ to create the unity. However, the bishops were fully satisfied with meeting once a year, eating lunch together, and discussing a few problems without ever taking the next step. I think Metropolitan Antony was not satisfied with that. He wanted to go forward and create real unity here, although he knew it would be very difficult.[7]

[7]Ibid.

However, Antony Bashir's frugality sabotaged his opportunity to lead the Standing Conference towards an American Orthodox Church. Because he refused to spend the money to hire office staff, he lacked the time necessary to lead SCOBA towards unity. His sister Adele remembered the discipline he imposed on himself: "He never cared to hire a full-time secretary, because he was used to getting help whenever he needed it, and besides, he wanted to do the work himself."[8] His workday routinely lasted from 8 A.M. to 7 P.M. During these hours, he worked either in his office or in the basement of the house he shared with Adele. "In the daytime he did not talk to me; I hardly talked to him. Both of us knew what we had to do."[9] Fr Schmemann reflected:

I think he could have been a greater power in the Standing Conference, but again, it was always the same. He was always rushing home to prepare packages of books and so on. This is where I saw his weakness: for him to save fifty cents on stamps or not pay someone to help him was more important than to spend time on creating one Church in America. He would be quite bold in his calls for unity, but there was no follow up, because then he would return to his basement and do nothing towards creating a united Church.[10]

Paradox of Inconsistency

This inconsistency revealed itself in other areas as well, according to Fr Schmemann:

He was the same with his approach to ordinations. He was the greatest supporter of the idea that we needed educated clergy, that we needed a central school. At the same time, he would ordain anyone. Because a parish needed a priest, he would ordain any convert without any preparation, and that was his weakness. He

[8]Adele Khoury, personal interview.
[9]Ibid.
[10]Ibid.

saw the light, and he always proclaimed it to be true; but practically, he compromised much too often.[11]

The worst consequence of these personal weaknesses was the cost to the American Orthodox Church. Had he been willing to spend money—to hire an office staff, to delegate authority to others to carry out daily tasks, to finance an American Orthodox university and an American Orthodox seminary—he would have achieved a number of practical and important steps toward the creation of a full-fledged American Orthodox Church. These steps would have placed Antony in a position to lead SCOBA itself to take the next steps necessary for creating Orthodox unity in America.

Antony Bashir's Greatness

Antony's greatness, however, outweighed his weakness. Disappointment over what he failed to achieve, and sadness over opportunities lost, in no way diminish the greatness of that which he did achieve. Antony Bashir was a giant among men. He was a natural leader whose very presence commanded respect. Fr Schmemann noted that what he saw in Metropolitan Antony differed from what he saw in other bishops:

> My impression of Antony Bashir is a very unique one, because we, in this country, are used to a lack of leadership among the bishops. They follow, rather than lead their churches. The feeling you had with Metropolitan Antony was that he was truly in command in many ways—not totally, not entirely—but in many ways. At his invitation, I attended with him several of the conventions of the Antiochian Archdiocese. This was the most revealing experience I had. At one convention, when I arrived, he said: "Here, Fr Schmemann has come, and I, being the Metropolitan, can overrule all the decisions of this convention. Therefore, I rule that there will be not be any such-and-such, even though it is listed on the program." They heard him make the rule, and no

[11]Ibid.

one protested. Can you imagine that? In any other convention there would have been a motion, a vote, a this and a that; but he *said* it, and it was so.[12]

Knowing how to lead and having a commanding presence can, in the wrong hands, lead to a dictatorial tyranny. In the person of Antony Bashir, however, the mystery of the Church spoken of by St Ignatius of Antioch was achieved: "Therefore, it is fitting for you to run your race together with the bishop's purpose, as you do. For your presbytery, worthy of fame and worthy of God, is attuned to the bishop like strings to a lyre. Therefore, by your unity and harmonious love, Jesus Christ is sung."[13]

This fact is further evident from Fr Schmemann's remarks about Metropolitan Antony's interactions with his flock:

The difference between him and many other bishops I saw was that he transformed the convention into a kind of family affair. He impressed me because he seemed to know everyone by name. It wasn't an anonymous relationship—bishop, then priest, then somewhere laity. He knew practically every member of the Archdiocese, or at least those of a certain age, by name. And that is something very special and evangelical.

One felt that the man was not a functionary. It was his church; he was its bishop. He never had any idea that he might leave and do something else. He belonged to it totally, and there was a kind of organic unity between the bishop and the church; not perfect of course, but at least it was there. When you see bishops in the Russian Church being transferred—today he's in Chicago, tomorrow in San Francisco—and very easily changing a priest from one parish to another, and then you encounter Metropolitan Antony, you felt that this was not the case. That absolutely was his church, his family. He was the center of it, and that's all. I think, when I remember him, that is my feeling, that he was truly, organically connected with the church. Whether he used that power and that

12Ibid.
13*Epistle to the Ephesians*, 4

possibility to the full extent, whether his vision was always correct, that's another story. But that unity was there.[14]

No Other Life but the Church

St Paul's words apply as much to Antony Bashir as they do to everyone else: "We have this treasure in earthen vessels."[15] Antony Bashir had greatness mixed with personal weakness, but he was never a mean or vindictive man.

> I would even stress this point. For example, I, personally, very often had to argue and quarrel with him about dollars and cents, things like that. But it was never personal. And then he would take his big cigar and smile and say, "Fr Schmemann, you know . . ." He was not a petty man. He laughed at himself. Have you ever seen a bishop laughing at himself? I think that is a great sense of humility. He was a man who took himself with a kind of sense of humor. I think he was a great, very peculiar, original, and, in many ways, unique man. Deeply speaking, his real term of reference was very Christian. He wasn't at all a man of selfishness or self-centeredness. Even though he profited by the Church, he also belonged to it without any reservations. He had no other life. I think that is the essence of episcopacy: he had no other life but the Church—no personal friends, no anything, just the Church.[16]

[14]Ibid.
[15]2 Corinthians 4.7
[16]Schmemann, personal interview.

CHAPTER 12

Archbishop Michael Shaheen Speaks

The election and consecration of Michael Shaheen as a metropolitan and successor to Metropolitan Samuel David continued the division between Toledo and New York. That division was not healed in Metropolitan Antony's lifetime. However, Antony's successor, Metropolitan Philip Saliba, and Metropolitan Michael Shaheen were able to make peace and reunite the two archdioceses in June 1975.

In 1989, Archbishop Michael made an archpastoral visit to St Elijah parish in Oklahoma City. On the occasion of this visit, he gave an informal interview with the author, which was videotaped. The following is based upon a transcript of that interview.

Archbishop Michael, I am working on a book on the life of Metropolitan Antony Bashir. I wrote my thesis on him for graduation. It is only proper, since I will need to deal with the subject of New York and Toledo, that I speak with the person who was directly involved in that.

Archbishop Michael (AM): Yes, to get both sides of the story.

Saidna, could you speak about your early relationship with Metropolitan Antony Bashir?

AM: I was among the first group of students that Archbishop Antony prepared for the priesthood. I point back to 1950, not earlier. I never dreamt, never thought it would come true, that I would become a bishop in competition with my mentor, with my bishop. I think I've told the story many times concerning what I know about when Archbishop Samuel died.

After Archbishop Samuel died, the Diocese of Toledo was vacant for four years. Antony took about three or four churches from Toledo, but the rest resisted going to New York. We were in special convention in Los Angeles when Archbishop Samuel died. I was a priest along with Tom Ruffin and James Meena.

Word got out that Archbishop Samuel had died. Antony wanted to go to the funeral; he wanted to. But he wanted to sense their response. Would Toledo object or accept him? Toledo rejected him totally. Because one week earlier, before Archbishop Samuel died, Archbishop Antony had been in Toledo at St Elias Church, which belonged to the Archdiocese of New York. In his sermon he told the people of St Elias to have nothing to do with St George Cathedral anymore. St George Cathedral belonged to the Diocese of Toledo. He said, "Let them go their way; we will go our way."

So, one week later, Archbishop Samuel died. If Antony hadn't said those words from the pulpit—this is what the Toledo people told me later—they would have been happy to have him come, to preside at the funeral, and to all become one.

Had that happened, I wouldn't be a bishop today. This is the truth. But because Antony did what he did at St Elias Church, the Toledo people said, "In no way will we accept Archbishop Antony at the funeral. Anybody but Antony." So the Toledo people contacted the Holy Synod, and the Holy Synod sent three bishops to come and preside at the funeral. Mary Douad paid the whole bill (but that's beside the point).

In the meantime, the New York Archdiocese was still meeting in special convention in Los Angeles. Various people at the convention began saying, "Oh, Antony has been rejected by Toledo." Meena, Ruffin, and myself said, "You know what, why does a bishop have to wait for an invitation to go to a bishop's funeral? We think Antony should go on his own."

Meena and Ruffin looked at me and asked if I would tell this to Antony. I said, "I won't do it alone. If all of us go, then I will." So we went to Antony's room for an interview. I don't recall who opened it up, but anyway, we said, "Saidna, we think it's a bad mistake not to go to Toledo. If you go to Toledo and preside at his funeral, everything will be smooth. There will be one diocese again."

Antony replied, "I sent Fr Ellis Khoury there to feel them out, and Albert Khoury is working on it. They both say that if I go, Toledo will assault me, or they'll shoot me." We said, "We don't believe that. If you go, all of us will go with you." Antony said, "I'll let you know." The final verdict was . . . Albert Khoury is, as you know, a good politician, but he got scared. And Ellis Khoury said, "You'd better not come." As a result, Antony did not go, and three bishops came to serve the funeral. They buried Archbishop Samuel in Toledo.

Four years go by. Bishop Antony takes four churches from Toledo, but he couldn't get the rest. They stood and were strong. They were fighters, and they had money. Mary Douad and Joseph Joseph spent $100,000 or $200,000. They didn't want to go with Antony.

I still belonged to the Archdiocese of New York. I was in Montreal when Metropolitan Epiphanius came to visit in this country. We had instructions from Antony not to receive him. The parish put pressure on us by saying things like, "Abouna, he is a bishop. You have to show your respect." We were invited to have dinner with Epiphanius. "But we have instructions from our bishop," we said, trying to decline. "I want you to come to the dinner, and to the dinner you'll go."

Fr Theodore Ziton and myself went to the dinner. I'll never forget the time Epiphanius stood and said, "You two are good priests. I know your bishop told you not to come, and you should obey your bishop. But I'm glad I got to see you at the dinner and that you came out of courtesy." Epiphanius then said to me, "You would be a good man to go to Toledo, to be the bishop."

"Saidna, how could I? I cannot risk turning against Antony. It would have to be a decision of the Synod. I don't want to be a bishop that badly." Mary Douad and Joseph Joseph asked, "Would you be our bishop?" I said, "Only under one circumstance—if elected by the Holy Synod and the patriarch. I will not rebel against Antony."

So then, later, I got a telegram: "You have been elected Bishop of Toledo." The Holy Synod had to choose from three names, but they knew automatically they were electing me. Antony was there. Metropolitan Boulos was there. Epiphanius had an argument with Antony. He told Antony, "There's a diocese that is vacant; they want their bishop."

When Antony saw that they didn't have a majority, he said, "Well, who is he?" Epiphanius said, "I'm going to nominate Archimandrite Shaheen from Montreal." Antony agreed with this, according to Metropolitan Boulos, one hundred per cent. It was a unanimous vote. There was not one dissenting vote on the Synod.

That's when the patriarch wired me. The telegram said, "You have been elected." I thought it was a joke, like the one Fr Theodore Ziton and I did on somebody when we were young priests. In a couple of days we found out that it is no joke. I started getting calls from the Syrian-Arabic newspapers of New York and Los Angeles. But you have to let them know you accept. So I sent a wire: "I accept."

I went to the Holy Synod with Antony. Antony had contacted me. "Get ready, we'll go together." I got on the same plane with Archbishop Antony. I had an uncle from Canada, and I had a doctor, my cousin, who went with us. Mary Douad was also on the same flight as we left from New York.

What can I tell you? We got off the plane, talking all the time, you know. Mary Douad was happy. The archbishop said, "Don't let them deceive you. Don't let them tell you this or that. They need to know their bishop is my bishop."

We got to the Beirut International Airport. Five or six bishops met us in reception. They were there to pick up Bashir. I don't recall what happened. I don't think I went with Antony. Anyhow, the Synod was held.

You know what they do when they elect a bishop? After you have wired your consent and have arrived, the bishops go into session. You're outside. You carry a candle. You're escorted to the Synod meeting. You stand. The patriarch says, "Come forward, come forward, come forward." It is a beautiful ceremony. This is just the formal acceptance. They ask you, "What have you come here for?" I said, "I have come in obedience to the decision of the Holy Synod that has elected me, humbly to serve the Church." And you give your verbal acceptance.

From there on you cannot leave the patriarch. For three days we stayed there and prepared for Sunday morning. I remember I had ulcers. That's why I said, "Saidna, can't I stay at the hotel, and I'll come back." "No, you have to stay." "But you know I have to eat something every two hours like milk or crackers. Whatever it takes to keep the stomach going."

On Sunday morning I was consecrated at the Church of the Holy Cross. Antony and Epiphanius were my sponsors. They put their hands on me and took me around the altar three times. We had twelve bishops, six on the one side, six on the other. It was a beautiful ceremony. I had to declare that I believe the Nicene Creed and had to write it out in my own handwriting. You can't type it out. "I, the son of George Shaheen, from such and such an area, hereby declare to the Holy Synod that I believe in one God, the Father Almighty," and so on. And at the end it says that I will always obey till my last days the decisions of the Holy Ecumenical Councils, the decisions of the regional councils and all the decisions of the Holy Synod of Antioch. Then at the bottom I wrote my signature.

After the ceremony we had a big dinner with catered lamb. I remember how cooperative everyone was. We spent a little time there waiting on the proxies. I can't go to Toledo without them. I was asked, "Bishop of Toledo, what does that mean? Are you equal to the rest? Or are you under Antony?" I said, "I don't know."

Anyway, Antony made a proclamation saying that I was elected the bishop of Toledo to serve the Diocese of Toledo under Archbishop Bashir. Others said, "We'll see what we can do later."

What was I to do? Am I going to say no? No, I came back to Montreal. The Toledo people said, "We would like to meet you, but we are not ready to receive you. But we want to meet you." So I went to Toledo.

In Toledo I was told, "Saidna, you were our choice. We want you as our leader. But we cannot, under any circumstances, accept anything less than what Archbishop Samuel was." I asked, "What's the reason?" Here's what they said: "Number one, if we accept you as a bishop, it reflects on Archbishop Samuel that he was not a metropolitan. We would become illegal all these years. If nothing else, accept that. Number two, Archbishop Antony misused us, pushed us around. And one week before our bishop died, he excommunicated us and had nothing to do with us." I said, "Well, in that case we'll communicate, we'll talk again."

I left and went back to Montreal and spent two months as bishop there. Of course the people in Montreal were good to me. They bought me a set of vestments that I still use to this day.[1] Pure gold with a crown. They honored me with banquets and dinners, everything.

Finally, after two months, Antony held a board of trustees meeting in Montreal. During the meeting, he said, "Well, Saidna, we want you to go to Toledo. You are an able man. Do what it takes. Don't mention my name in your services.[2] Try and gain these people. We want to become one. You're from a good family. You're this and you're that."

I told him, "Yes, absolutely Saidna. I'll be glad to try." Do you remember Abdallah Khoury? He was there. I said, "Saidna, I'll take Toledo." As God is my witness, I then said to Abdallah, "Don't interfere. You're the one that caused the problem with Toledo many years ago."

You know what Abdallah did? He stood up, yelled, "You can't talk to me like that. What did I do? I killed myself for the church," and he walked out. He was the main cause of the split that created the Toledo problem in the first place. Abdallah Khoury and Richard Joseph originally were both members of St George in Toledo. St George was the first church in Toledo. St George was there twenty years before they had a second church. Richard Joseph stayed at St George and Abdallah Khoury helped build St Elias.

I didn't know what to do. I couldn't stay in Montreal. They had already gotten another priest, Fr Michael Howard. I ended up going to live with my parents in Canton, Ohio. Fr Howard drove me back to Toledo and on to Canton, Ohio.

My family was upset. I served a good month there. My message? I'm a bishop without a diocese, without a territory. It's God's truth, you know. My uncle is a very good friend of Antony. He and Antony played cards. They were the closest of friends. So my uncle said to

---

[1]Sometime after the death of Archbishop Michael Shaheen, these gold vestments were given by Bishop Demetri to St Elijah Orthodox Church in Oklahoma City, OK, where they are on display in the church's Historical Room.

[2]Not mentioning Antony in the Divine Services would give the impression that Shaheen and Bashir were equals.

Antony, "What did you do with my nephew, the happy Montreal priest?" Antony told him, "They elected him a bishop. They wanted him to be a bishop. I don't need a bishop." "What do you expect him to do?" my uncle asked. Antony replied, "That's his problem. He should go to Toledo. He is the bishop of Toledo. They have to accept him."

In other words, Antony wanted me to go to Toledo and clash with these people. If he didn't dare go there for the funeral, he thinks I'm going to go to Toledo!? The people in Toledo contacted the patriarch. They were told there was a solution. "Tell him to pack his bags and go back to Damascus. Have him tell the patriarch, 'You made me a bishop, where am I going to be located?' "

I went back to Brooklyn and told them the whole story. I was told, "Antony does not want you even if they don't get a bishop in Toledo. He doesn't need a bishop."

So the Holy Synod invited Antony, but Antony refused to go because he knew what was coming up. The Holy Synod cited the proxies, "Whereas there was a vacancy in Toledo; and whereas there was Metropolitan Archbishop Samuel David who was consecrated and died on such a day; and whereas there was a need for a successor, for a shepherd, we hereby declare Bishop Michael Shaheen to be named metropolitan, successor to Samuel David, based on the fact that the Archdiocese of Toledo was not created by a decision of the Holy Synod, but was an Archdiocese *de facto.*" It's a Latin term meaning, "it's there." Whether you make a decision or not, it's still there.

Therefore they offered me this *praxis* (a *praxis* gives a bishop his rights, a bishop has rights). They gave me my *praxis.* Then the news comes to Toledo. The newspapers say Metropolitan Michael has been elected by the Holy Synod and named to the Toledo Diocese. They said that Antony's position had not been accepted; and that for some mysterious reason, the Synod reconvened and discussed this matter and did this act.

I had no choice. I arrived in Toledo to a big celebration. All the churches came to receive us at the airport. Robert Shaheen's mother was at the airport dancing and celebrating. What was she dancing about? The bishop is her relative. And from there on out, it's history.

Saidna, could you speak about Metropolitan Antony Bashir's relationship with Metropolitan Samuel David?

AM: Archbishop Samuel David, Monsour Laham, Archbishop Antony, and Mary Douad met in Boston. They agreed that each one would run his own territory. Later, in one of our Archdiocese conventions, they agreed that whoever died first, the other would become the single head of a united archdiocese. I remember at the convention, someone from the floor, somebody objected. Antony got angry and said, "We're discussing our death, and you can't agree?"

Archbishop Samuel and Archbishop Antony served together many, many times. They served together in my ordinations.

If the relationship between Antony and Samuel continued to get better and better, what was it that caused Antony to break his relationship with Samuel David and Toledo?

AM: The office of Archbishop of New York was also recognized as a metropolitan by the Holy Synod. This meant the Archbishop of New York, because he was a metropolitan, had a seat on the Holy Synod. When Antony and Samuel made their agreement, the Archbishop of Toledo was not a metropolitan and therefore did not have a seat on the Holy Synod.

But Archbishop Samuel donated toward the patriarchal office and donated towards the Balamand. It's in the books and the records; he directed all of the proceeds, and it went to the Patriarchate. Therefore the patriarch said, "Even though there is no decision, he will be called metropolitan, due to his gracious Christian deeds and charities."

Therefore Archbishop Samuel David is made a metropolitan and makes his first visit to the old country as a metropolitan. It was the issue of Archbishop Samuel being made a metropolitan that upset Archbishop Bashir. That's why he broke with Archbishop Samuel and Toledo one week before Archbishop Samuel died.

After the death of Archbishop Samuel, while I was still a priest in Montreal, Archbishop Antony visited me. I remember he had a hole in his T-shirt and I said, "Saidna, you need a new T-shirt." He said, "What does that mean? That's material stuff. Don't worry about it.

You know I made a bad mistake once." I replied, "You don't make mistakes." He said, "I stood at St Elias, and from the pulpit I broke all relations with Toledo. I was angry. I shouldn't have done that." I said, "You didn't know what the consequences would be." He said, "I wish I hadn't spoken so fast."

Archbishop Michael, Metropolitan Antony died twenty-four years ago. What is your impression of Antony after all these years?

AM: Archbishop Antony was a very eloquent spokesman for the church. He was a very impressive man who knew much psychology. Before you spoke, he knew almost what you were going to say. He could read your expressions. He could handle people here in the parishes so very well. He had them in the palm of his hand. He was an intelligent man. His command of the Arabic and English languages was excellent.

You know that Gibran, Khalil Gibran . . . When Antony was a priest he translated Gibran from English to Arabic. When Gibran heard about it he said, "Who is this priest that dares translate what I write?" So they told him about this priest that goes around from city to city preaching and selling books.

Antony wrote Gibran a letter. "I would like to come and see you and let you examine my translations." Antony went and visited Gibran. Gibran liked Antony and gave him a few tips on the translations. Gibran liked Antony, because Antony was willing to be corrected. And Gibran told Antony, "Go ahead and continue your work." Antony translated all the work of Gibran into the Arabic language.

Archbishop Antony was very talented and shrewd. He knew how to handle people very, very well. I recall being at a big dinner in Canton, Ohio. I wasn't a bishop. Antony said, "Here's to your becoming a bishop." I thought to myself, "Boy, he knows how to compliment people."

Before I became a priest, before Antony ordained me, he asked me, "Do you want to get married or don't you?" I said, "I don't really have anybody. I'm not thinking about it, about getting married. I thought I'd serve the church." "That's a very wise decision," Antony said, "who needs kids, who needs a wife? Who needs waaa, waaa, waaa. Be free to travel."

This is really what I wanted to do. But my family said to me, "Isn't it sad what Antony said? Life's too short. You're still young. Why don't you get married like everyone else?" So I told them, "Gee, let me think about it some more."

Archbishop Antony was not perfect. None of us are perfect. He was very conservative. One time I wrote him by airmail. He wrote me back and said, "What? You have too much money? The regular mail is not good enough for you?"

He was very efficient. He answered his mail immediately. He never went to bed without answering all his mail on his own typewriter in Arabic and English. He typed all the certificates, all the letters, everything by hand on an old fashioned typewriter. It's amazing how much work he did. He had an American priest as a secretary who did some typing for him at the end because his fingers started to hurt. He had written so much in his lifetime, that one of his fingers was crooked.

You should ask the first seminarians that were studying in New York. They would come see him on weekends. He would save all the books that had to be mailed out of the house. He would put them in a basket, like a supermarket basket, and tell them to take them by the post office. So a bunch of them would take them, and he wouldn't give them any money for the stamps. He would look at me and say, "It's your turn." And so I would pay for the stamps.

Yes, he was very conservative. I remember serving my first Divine Liturgy with him after I was consecrated a bishop. We were in Montreal. I had these beautiful gold vestments.[3] Russian priests made them in New York from material imported from France. Genuine gold with a beautiful crown. Back then they cost $2,000, and the crown another thousand. The vestments were a gift from my church. I was serving my first liturgy with him in Montreal. He looked at me and said, "What's that?" "It was a little gift from my parish. They liked me and insisted on giving the vestments to me," I told him. He replied, "They're too expensive, too expensive. Look at my vestments. My sis-

[3]See Note 212 above.

ter made them. It cost me $200." Actually his vestments were sewn crooked. But he was very conservative. He liked to say, "It doesn't mean anything, all this materialism."

I remember complaining to Archbishop Antony a couple of times. I told him we would like to have him come visit us every year. "But," I said, "you stipulate you want a $250 honorarium plus a hotel room, and our people have a big fight here every time. 'What do we want the bishop for? He insists on getting money from a few people.' So we have a big fight amongst the board, and it divides the parish."

And Antony replied, "You know, I don't have to come here, and they don't have to pay me. But some day, these people that accuse me of asking for money and demanding they pay for my trip, some day they are going to bless my memory because I'm going to leave all that money to the church." He never bought a suit, never bought a coat. Everything was donated. He knew exactly where the families were. He'd have me call them up. They had his measurements, too. It was part of his nature.

Could you tell us the story of Antony's visit to the Holy Synod at the golden anniversary of the Patriarch of Antioch?

AM: One hundred bishops from all over the world came. Now the patriarchs didn't come. They sent representatives. They were all seated according to seniority. The Patriarch of Constantinople's representative in front on the right and on the left Alexandria, Russia, all of them were there. I went with Antony as a priest. They all spoke. Some of them had translators. They gave him all kind of honors, including from the University of Greece. The whole evening was dedicated to the patriarch.

Antony's speech was very short. First he said (it went something like this), "If you have something and you add to it, you're to be commended. But when we create something out of nothing, you're to be praised, and honored and elevated. Our patriarch has built a beautiful patriarchate. But they have a lousy dining room. But where's the money? You know, money is the muscle of life. On behalf of my beloved brother, Metropolitan Samuel David, and myself, we will donate $50,000 towards a new Grand Salon."

We had stipulations. Antony said, "You build; you send me the bills." And we built it. Eventually it was built. It was a favorite saying of his, "Money is the muscle of life."

Once you were consecrated a bishop and became the metropolitan of Toledo, were there any efforts made at reconciliation?

AM: The only effort that was made was by Mr B. D. Eddy of Oklahoma City. He wrote to Antony and myself and said, "We've got to end this. There has to be a way out. I want to get you together and make peace." I, of course, answered him in a very positive way: "I'm ready to meet anywhere it takes, at any time. I'll meet Antony." I don't know exactly what took place, but we never met. I am discussing only the positive things. Whatever is negative I don't want to deal with. I'll let history judge who's right and who's wrong.

As a metropolitan, you had your own vote in the Holy Synod, as did Antony. What was it like sitting on the Holy Synod together?

AM: Archbishop Antony went back one time. We were in this huge salon. Bishops were sitting all the way around this huge table. I was on one side, and I had two pre-delegates, lay delegates, with me. And he had a lawyer with him. We had a couple of good lawyers, too, and they were arguing back and forth over technical points.

One of the bishops surprised everybody and asked for the floor, Archbishop of Hama. He said, "Excuse me, I have to talk. Saidna, I had an aunt call me. She told me about a Mr Mielke of Detroit. He used to be a big man, but he had an accident. The man told my aunt, 'Antony used to know me. He used to come to my house in Detroit. But because I had this accident, and I'm not a millionaire anymore, I don't see him anymore. This bishop looks after me. And we can use three bishops next year.' "

Antony got very angry and lost his temper and said, "I will never accept this decision as long as I live. Nobody will divide North America." He talked very rough and used, I don't know, abusive language that day. I say abusive language and by that I mean tough, tough language within the Synod. The patriarch said, "Stop!" It was the first time I ever saw anything like this. "You don't talk that way to him or in front of the Synod." That calmed him down. And after that meeting, Antony never attended another meeting. He boycotted.

I never saw Antony or spoke to him again. When he died, I went and paid my respects. I admired the man.

Saidna, how was it that you and Antony's successor, Metropolitan Philip Saliba, were able to achieve reconciliation and unite together into one archdiocese?

AM: Archbishop Philip Saliba visited me along with Fr George Rados and Fr George Khoury. They were in Toledo for their SOYO Convention. They came on the Sunday afternoon after the convention.[4] I was hurt that week. You know, I was a bishop at home. I said, "Couldn't they have at least called? I don't have to go to their convention and be embarrassed." It felt like I was being ignored. And I said, "Well, God will provide a way." And the phone rang. The voice on the other end asked, "Would you receive Metropolitan Saliba as a visitor socially?" Now all my people knew they had boycotted us. But I said, "Sure, why not?"

I put some coffee on. They came over. I remember I presented him with a nice icon, a little gift, a gesture of good will. We discussed reconciliation. I said, "Saidna, I might as well tell you, Toledo will never, never, never join you. And I doubt if New York will join Toledo." He said, "But those two words have to be dropped."

Saliba asked me, "What else do you think?" I said, "I have a vote in the Synod. I can't give that up. If I give that up, I'm saying that all the pastors are wrong or illegal or whatever. So what do you lose if we have one archdiocese with two votes? Gives us more prestige." He said, "That will always leave the door open for division." We worked it out by saying, "If he doesn't go vote, then I can go vote." We would represent each other, and that resolved it.

I had liked what Philip had said once. I read it in a magazine. Philip had given a speech in Charleston, West Virginia, in which he said,

[4]Fr Antony Gabriel was at St Elias at this time, but was in the hospital. He had several meetings with Archbishop Michael and the Joseph family. Once permission for a meeting had been given, Fr Gabriel communicated this information to Metropolitan Philip Saliba.

"We must be united. Because someday the next generation will come and spit on our graves because of the kind of bishops we were." I said to Philip, "Why don't we bury the past and start again, rather than have the past bury us and get us like everybody else?" He liked that.

So he said, "You appoint a committee, and I'll appoint a committee and let them discuss the various details." And he left. I had Fr John Stefan, I think. He had George Khoury and Rados. Rados was reasonable but Khoury was not. But then, after months and months and months, it kept getting worse and worse.

Finally I met Philip in Pittsburgh. I said, "Do you like the basic principles?" He said, "What do you want to do, two metropolitans?" I said, 'No, you keep the name metropolitan, and I will keep the name archbishop." We agreed, and the lawyers agreed, "There's nothing wrong with that; it sounds good." Thank God, we got it worked out.

What was the response of the Patriarch and the Holy Synod to the reconciliation of New York and Toledo?

AM: By 1975, when the reunification took place, Metropolitan Elias had been elected the new patriarch and became Patriarch Elias IV. So Elias IV was the patriarch when reconciliation was made between Toledo and New York. Saliba and I were in the old country at the Holy Synod. Elias IV was the one who announced to the Synod that America has won. All the bishops clapped and said again and again in Arabic, "The angels in heaven are singing. The angels in heaven are singing." The patriarch raised his hand, and everyone quieted down when he said, "Come on back down to earth."

The patriarch took off two *engolpia* and put one on me and one on Saliba. Everyone started taking pictures. And the word got out. We were on the front page of every newspaper. And Minor George was there. No, not Minor, Rudy George. Rudy George had Saliba and I stand together and take pictures so that things would be good in the church.

Saidna, if we could return to Antony for a moment. I interviewed Antony's younger sister. She told me when Antony translated Gibran's writings, he would give the translation to her. She would then read it out loud back to him, sometimes five, six, seven times. As she read, if there is a mistake, he would correct it. It had to sound just right to his ears. She said she used to sit for hours and hours and hours until he was satisfied with the message itself. He wanted to strive for the best.

AM: That's why his Arabic writing was the best. It has a certain rhythm, a certain rhythm to it. They're easier to read, to understand. I asked him once, when we were on our way to a funeral, "When you deliver a sermon, which is easier for you, English or Arabic?" He said that Arabic was much easier for him, but he spoke well in English, too.

Antony was very bold. He came to Canton, Ohio, where he always got a large room in a hotel owned by an Italian, Mr. Onesto. Antony traveled all the time, and he got mixed up. He thought Onesto was Greek. "Hello, Mr. Onesto." "Hello, your Highness." "I just got back from Greece. I flew over Athens. What a beautiful city that is." He was trying to impress the man. He was hoping to get an upgrade to a suite. But Onesto was Italian. He wasn't Greek.

I remember when we were in convention in Los Angeles and Archbishop Samuel died. Fr Tom Ruffin was there. Fr James Meena was there. He decided not to go to the funeral. The local parish priest in Los Angeles said to Archbishop Antony, "Do you want to stay here for two extra days? We would be glad to pay for it." "What do you mean, pay for it?" Antony asked. "The parish said if you would like to stay a few days more and rest, it's no problem; you're welcome to it," the parish priest replied. Antony says, "I don't need that. Get me the manager. I want to teach you a lesson. I want everyone to be clear on this."

He picked up the phone and spoke with the manager. He told him what a great hotel it was, what a great convention we had had, our success is due to your wonderful facilities, thank you for your kindness, for this and for that. Then he added, "Do you mind if I stay a few more days? Would it be possible to comp my rooms?" The manager said, of course Bashir can stay, and he would be happy to comp his rooms. Bashir hung up the phone and said to us, "This is how you do it. Learn a lesson, each one of you."

He had a way of doing it. I wouldn't dare do that. He impressed all the bishops when he went to the old country. He was a good talker;

he gave them good times. One time he visited the patriarch until 1:00 in the morning. He had all the bishops and the patriarch listening to him tell about his experiences. He had a lot to say.

Saidna, do you have any funny stories to tell about Antony, stories that give us a glimpse of him as a man?

AM: On a Sunday in the old country, a certain lady came up and showed a special interest in Antony. "Oh, Saidna, I love you. I haven't seen you in so many years." She went on and on. As we were leaving Antony said to me, "Imagine, she had a crush on me, and I almost married her many years ago. Only imagine what I would be like today . . ." It was so funny. He was a funny man, very funny.

Quebec, Canada, is a historic site to see, about one hundred miles from Montreal. We had two families there, the Shewaides. Sy Shewaide was a wealthy man who liked elegant things. Antony knew these people, knew exactly what to say and when to say it. So he used to pay a visit to Sy Shewaide's home. He usually received a monetary gift for coming. So one time Antony visited him, but Antony didn't want to spend too much time because there were some big problems he needed to attend to. But he wanted to see Sy, pay his respects, maybe have a brief lunch with him, and come back to Montreal. But Sy wanted Bashir to stay longer. Sy said, "I want to take you for a ride." "Where to?" Bashir asked. "I want to take you to the zoo." "The zoo? Why? I live at a zoo!"

On another occasion, he visited this lady several days in a row. Each day she fed him watercress sandwiches. On the third day he tells her, "You know what? Don't bother cooking anymore. Just put a rope around my neck and tie me outside." I loved it.

Bashir used to drink a lot. Not to the extent of getting drunk. But he had to have a little *arak* to keep going. Now this was during Prohibition. Bashir, the sheriff, and another person went to Akron. They would buy a half gallon or a gallon of *arak*. They had their connections. One time they went and bought two bottles. I don't know if they were half gallons or full gallons; they were two big jugs. They put them in the trunk of the car. They were coming from Akron to Canton. The light changed and they stopped suddenly at a red light. There was a crash in the trunk; something broke. So they both got out and opened the trunk and saw one of the bottles was busted. Antony immediately said, "Too bad it was yours that broke." He was so sharp, so quick. I loved that. Antony loved telling his stories.

I remember going with my father to visit Antony in Brooklyn. My father wanted me to be a priest, but I didn't want to be a priest. So my dad said, "Let's go see the bishop." So we went from Albany to Brooklyn. We got lost on the subway, and we were so hungry. When we got there, the bishop had already had his lunch and was having coffee. We sat outside on the balcony while he smoked his cigar. We spent about two hours. All I had had that day was a little grape juice. I was so hungry. He was not really generous.

AM: No, I don't remember ever eating at his house. Once his sister, Adele, put me in a room on the third floor. There was a wind coming in every once in a while, when the wind gusted. I tried to fall asleep. But the wind was rattling the door. Squeak. Squeak. Squeak. I got up to try and stop it. I finally put the shutter behind it.

As Archbishop Michael Shaheen concluded the interview, my two sons, Constantine and Philip, came in and briefly spoke with him. My sons liked him and joyfully asked, "When are you coming back?" The archbishop smiled warmly and said to them, "When the bishop comes we say, 'Blessed is he who comes in the name of the Lord.' And after he has been with us for three days we say, 'Blessed is he when he leaves!' I hope to see you in a couple of years.'" As he walked out of the room, Philip remarked, "He's a nice man."

This interview proved to be the only occasion that Archbishop Michael Shaheen would visit Oklahoma City. He fell asleep in the Lord on October 24, 1992.

CHAPTER 13

Metropolitan Philip
Saliba's Reflections

After the death of Metropolitan Antony Bashir, the widowed Archdiocese of New York needed to elect a successor. The Patriarch of Antioch appointed Metropolitan Ilyas Kurban as the *locum tenems* to oversee the archdiocese and to supervise the election of a successor. Nominations were made and an election held. Archimandrite Philip Saliba was chosen as metropolitan-elect. On Sunday, August 14, 1966, in St Elias Monastery in Dhour Schweer, Lebanon, he was consecrated as metropolitan archbishop for the Archdiocese of New York and all North America, by His Beatitude Patriarch Theodosius VI of Antioch and all the East.[1]

A few years prior to his death, Antony Bashir became seriously concerned about the future of the archdiocese. His sister remarked that "Antony used to mention Archimandrite Gregory Aboud and Fr Philip Saliba at the breakfast table. As you already know, he was grooming Philip for the future, but he never thought that he would die soon."[2] Antony took steps to cultivate good men who could serve well if chosen to be his successor. It was apparent that Metropolitan Antony held these clergy in high regard.

Philip Saliba had been ordained by Antony Bashir and had served him as one of his priests. Now, for over forty years, Metropolitan Philip has served as Antony's successor. St Paul said in his letter to the Corinthians, "I laid a foundation, and another is building upon it."[3]

[1] *The Word* 10. 6–7 (June-September 1966): 3.
[2] Adele Khoury, personal interview.
[3] 1 Corinthians 3.10.

In the same way, Antony Bashir laid the foundation for the Antiochian Archdiocese, and Metropolitan Philip has built upon that foundation. More than anyone else, Metropolitan Philip has a unique perspective from which to assess the strengths and weaknesses of Antony Bashir. He can evaluate what it was like to serve as a priest under Antony's leadership, and he knows what it was like to inherit the archdiocese that Antony had created. In February 2007, in Fort Lauderdale, Florida, Metropolitan Philip discussed Antony Bashir from this distinct perspective.[4]

When did you first meet Metropolitan Antony Bashir?

MP: I want to commend you on undertaking this study about my predecessor, the late Metropolitan Antony Bashir, who played a tremendous role in the development of our Church in North America. Before I came to this country, I really did not know him that well. The first time I remember having a glimpse of him was in 1954, when he made a trip to the Middle East, to Syria and Lebanon. We were deacons at the Patriarchate in Beirut. We just looked at him. He was a very imposing figure: tall, handsome. But we did not have a chance to know him in depth because he was a very busy man, keeping his appointments with religious leaders and political leaders and others. So, I really did not know him until I came to the United States of America.

What did your fellow students at the Balamand think about him?

MP: Well, my fellow students at Balamand did not know about him. I read something about him when I was a student at Balamand because I was fond of literature, and I was an avid reader of literary magazines and books and so forth. I came across some books that Archimandrite Antony Bashir had translated from English to Arabic. I remember also the first translation of *The Prophet* by Khalil Gibran. Remember that Khalil Gibran wrote *The Prophet* in English, and it was translated into Arabic by Archimandrite Antony Bashir in those days in America. They had worked on the translation, Gibran and

---

[4]From a personal interview with Metropolitan Philip Saliba, held in Fort Lauderdale, FL in February, 2007.

Antony Bashir; they had worked on the translation in Boston at the Rahbahny house. The Rahbahnys used to tell me about the arguments between Gibran and Bashir on language. Gibran was not a scholar of the Arabic language; his English was very strong, but his Arabic was not that strong. Bashir's Arabic was stronger than Gibran's.

When you came to the United States, what courtesies did Metropolitan Antony extend to you?

MP: Courtesies? None! I came to this country invited by the late Archbishop Samuel David of Toledo, Ohio, and went straight to the Holy Cross Theological School in Boston as a student belonging to the diocese of Samuel David. In January 1956 we arrived, I and another deacon, Emile Hannah. So we did not have much to do at that time with Metropolitan Antony, although we had students who belonged to the Archdiocese of New York studying there, such as the Archpriests George Shaheen, George Rados, Thomas Ruffin, and Gregory Ofiesh.

How did you come to Metropolitan Antony's attention, and how did you come to be under his jurisdiction?

MP: Well, it is a very strange circumstance, I would say. While at the Holy Cross Seminary in Boston, we Antiochian students were permitted to take our classes in English. The Greek students were not allowed to take their classes in English, but only in Greek. So we were getting very, very good grades. We Antiochians were getting very good grades, contrary to the Greek students who were struggling. They had been born in this country, and Greek was not their native language. English was. So they were struggling with the Greek language. There was a kind of murmuring in the school, "Why do the Antiochians take their classes in English, and we have to take our classes in Greek?"

Bishop Athenagoras was the dean of the Seminary; later on he was archbishop of the Greek Archdiocese of London and England. At the end of the academic year, the dean and the board of trustees of the Greek seminary passed a resolution to stop teaching anyone in English, saying that all of us should learn Greek. The Antiochian students under the omophore of Metropolitan Antony decided to leave and go to St Vladimir's Seminary. This left only Fr Emile and myself, who were under Archbishop David.

Archbishop David had a special love for the Greek seminary because of a lady from Worcester, Massachusetts, by the name of Mary Douad, who was a philanthropist for the Greek seminary, and she wanted us to stay there at the seminary. Emile and I discussed the situation, and we agreed to meet with Archbishop David and tell him this: "If we wanted to study Greek, we could have gone to Athens, we could have gone to Halki." But we did not want to study in any Greek country; we wanted to come to America. And since we came to America, we wanted to study theology in English, because this is the language that we were going to use to preach to people, our parishioners in the future—in English, not Greek. We had offers to go to Greece, to Halki, to Athens, to Salonica, to Moscow, to study in Russia, but I did not because I was in England, and I like the Anglo-Saxon mentality and approach to education.

So we met with the late Archbishop David, and told him we would like to join the rest of the Antiochian students and go to St Vladimir's Seminary and continue our theological study in English. His answer to us was, "You have three options: either to go back to the old country, to Lebanon and Syria; or to stay here at the Greek seminary and study in Greek; or to be ordained priests and serve parishes."

Emile and I discussed these options, and we did not accept any of them. So our answer to the late Archbishop Samuel, whom we loved very much because he was a very simple and good man with a beautiful voice, was that we do not accept any of these options. We are not going back to the old country, and we are not going to stay and study Greek in this institution, and we are not going to be ordained before we finished our theological education. When we told him that, he said, "You're on your own."

So Emile Hannah left and went to Charleston, West Virginia, to live with his aunt and with his cousin, Philip Haddad. And I left and went to the city of Boston. I rented a room and I worked. I worked that summer. I worked three days in a restaurant. After a few days, they fired me because they thought I was working too slowly. Then a parishioner of St John of Damascus by the name of John Stevens gave me a job in his factory. He used to manufacture skirts for women, and my job was to put a belt in every skirt and hang them in the factory.

So I worked for him, and he was paying me fifty dollars a week. That helped me to pay for my room until the end of summer. I applied to a few universities. I was accepted and encouraged to go to Detroit, to serve as a deacon at St George in Detroit and attend Wayne State University. I had a scholarship to Wayne State University because I had good grades from England.

And that's how you ended up with Metropolitan Antony. Which metropolitan ordained you as a priest?

MP: I was ordained a priest March 1, 1959, in Cleveland, Ohio, by Metropolitan Antony Bashir.

What was it like serving as a priest under Metropolitan Antony? How would you characterize his relationship with you and your relationship with him?

MP: Our relationship was mutual love and mutual respect. I respected the man a great deal after I got to know him when I was in Detroit. He used to visit Detroit, and I got to know him very well when he came. He was a very, very hard-working man. He knew the Archdiocese very well. He grew the archdiocese since he came to this country in the early 1920s.

He used to call me on the phone, and I called him in Brooklyn. He always called me collect, by the way, because he was very careful with his money. I received his calls, and he was a very, very beloved individual, beloved person, not only by me, but by my parishioners. He was always welcomed by the community.

Somewhere in the archives there was a note from Antony encouraging you to take a sabbatical and further your studies at St Vladimir's. How did you feel about this? Do you think he was preparing you for something? Did you attach any special significance to his wanting you to attend St Vladimir's?

MP: Well, it is true that he encouraged me to finish my studies. I needed some credits to finish my degree. He wanted me to get a degree in theology. I took a sabbatical leave from St George in Cleveland and went to St Vladimir's. My main interest was the Eucharist in the early Church. I did some research on the subject, which I loved very much. Of course, in those days, Fr Schmemann was teaching liturgical theology. He was a very, very gifted and eloquent lecturer and funny at the same time. You would never get bored in his classes. Liturgical theology was my favorite subject in school, and I did lots of research about the liturgy, about the Eucharist in the early Church.

Metropolitan Antony, I do not know what he really had in mind. My impression of him was that he did not want to see any other bishops serving with him. I can honestly say, for history's sake, that he thought he was going to live forever. He could not see another bishop serving with him. He wanted to be the only one; he was a one-man organization. He wanted to be the only archbishop over this archdiocese, contrary to what we have today.

But he never during your visits with him suggested . . . ? I know that bishops do focus on a person and try to encourage that person for a higher vision, a higher leadership, but that was not the case?

MP: No, except for once incident, again, for history's sake. In June, in my pastorate at St George in Cleveland, Ohio, Fr Ilyas Kurban (at that time he was the pastor of St George Church in Boston) and I came to New York City on a vacation. I think that was . . . I wanted to meet the late poet Elia Abu Madi. I read some of his poetry when I was a student in Lebanon and loved his poetry. Ilyas came from a village not very far from where I was born, called Al Muhaydafah.

I remember visiting him by myself; Kurban was not with me. I went to his office, and his office was downtown Brooklyn, a very humble place. I walked in, and he said, "Oh, you are Philip Saliba!" I wrote two or three articles to his paper, and he loved my Arabic language. So he said to me, "Well, you write beautiful Arabic." I said to him, "Thank you." He told me, "I am an old man, and I cannot publish this newspaper anymore. Why don't you take this newspaper? You take it and continue the *Asabeel* newspaper." This offer was great to me; I loved it because I always wanted to have a magazine and to publish things. I thought this was a great opportunity for me to do this.

So right away I went to visit Metropolitan Antony in Bayridge, and I told him about that. He screamed at me and said, "What are you trying to do? You want to publish an Arabic newspaper. Those who read Arabic are dead, most of them are dead. If you take this newspaper, you will starve to death." He had a tremendous sense of humor. He said to me, "You will starve to death. What do you want this job for, this newspaper? The Church needs you in the future." That's the only hint he ever mentioned to me about the future. Well, it did not mean that much to me in those days because I was pursuing my education.

Would you call Antony a visionary? Did he anticipate where the Orthodox Church in America is today? If so, what things did he do or initiate that helped the Church arrive where she is today?

MP: Well, of course Metropolitan Antony established many churches. I think when he became archbishop we had about thirty parishes in the archdiocese which were, most of them, established by Raphael Hawaweeny. Antony added another, I would say, thirty-five to thirty-six parishes to that number. When I was consecrated in 1966, we had about sixty-five parishes in the archdiocese. So Metropolitan Antony added lots of parishes to the archdiocese.

Antony felt very much at home in America. He spoke perfect English. He was a great orator . . . a great, great orator. He published *The Word* magazine. He resumed publication of *The Word* magazine in English in 1957. You see, it was published first in Arabic. The last issue was published by Emmanuel Abo-Hatab in 1931, and then it stopped publication until 1957, when Metropolitan Antony resumed publication of the work in the English language.

He used to edit *The Word* magazine. He used to put it together. I mean, he had no secretary, had nobody, and he was doing all this work by himself. He was traveling in North America from New York to California, from Montreal to Florida to Texas, traveling throughout this archdiocese. No one was at home except Adele, his sister. She took some phone calls, but he did all this work by himself.

I mean, he was an outstanding worker really. He did lots of work. He believed in English. He published many, many books. The late

Monsour Laham helped him a great deal to publish books, Sunday school books, in English. He established the book department in the archdiocese. He started selling books. We continue now to sell books. Of course we have expanded the book department a great deal.

Metropolitan Antony had a missionary spirit, although it was not that organized, and it was not that effective. He did not go to the Americans, to convert Americans to Orthodoxy. His main concern was to gather, as they called them at that time, the Syrians. Our archdiocese was called the Syrian Archdiocese until 1969, when I corrected the name and changed the word Syrian Archdiocese to the Antiochian Archdiocese, just to be faithful to history, because our Church was never called the Syrian Church. You see the Syriac Church is called the Syrian Church. As a matter of fact, the Syriacs in this country protested to us, "How come you are calling your archdiocese Syrian?" We are not the Syrian Archdiocese, after all; they are the Syrian Archdiocese. So in 1969—that is, three years after the death of Metropolitan Antony—I was determined to correct this historical error and to change the name Syrian to Antiochian. People from a Syrian background thought that I did not like Syria. But I love Syria; I love Lebanon. I am pan-Arab, you know. I believe in Arabism and so forth. So I told them, "No, I like them; we're trying to correct an historical error."

Was he visionary in terms of Orthodox unity?

MP: I would say yes, he was. In 1961, SCOBA was organized. And at the beginning of the constitution of SCOBA—and I don't have the constitution before me to quote exactly—I think in Article One under the purpose of SCOBA, one of the purposes of SCOBA was Orthodox unity. So he was mindful from that time of the future of Orthodoxy in this country. I do not know whether others, other bishops, other members of SCOBA, had the same vision as Metropolitan Antony.

Was he the first to extend a welcome to the Western Rite?

MP: No, the Western Rite movement started in Europe before it started here in America. It started in Europe, but let's just talk about America. The Western Rite people are Orthodox in their dogmas and doctrines and so forth. If you look at the Church before the Schism of 1054, we had many, many different expressions. Liturgies are cultural expressions. We in the East like the Byzantine Liturgy, John Chrysostom's liturgy, because of its beauty, ceremonies, etc. The West is not used to all these elaborate liturgies; they want simplicity, they want a simple liturgy. So we examined their liturgical texts and liturgical books and so forth. In dogmas and doctrines, they are Orthodox one hundred percent, but their liturgical expressions are different. They use the Western Rite Liturgy. And the Western Rite Liturgy is Orthodox also.

When the Church was one, the Church in the West was using a similar liturgy. In the East we were using a different liturgy, the Byzantine Liturgy, or the Syro-Byzantine Liturgy. You see, John Chrysostom was originally from Antioch, and Antioch was in Syria. When we speak about Byzantine music, I always call it Syro-Byzantine; so I will call it a Syro-Byzantine liturgy, you see. We in the East—I mean the Arabic Church, it is not a Byzantine Church but an Arabic Church— we adopted the Byzantine chants and the Byzantine hymns. Some of the authors were from Lebanon and Syria, like St Romanus and St John of Damascus, the author of the Octoechos and the eight tones and so forth. So the Western Rite in our archdiocese is a welcome expression of Western Christianity, but it is Orthodox one hundred percent.

Metropolitan Antony was close to Fulton Sheen and the Ecumenical Movement. Did he have a deep interest in ecumenism or was it only shallow?

MP: Ecumenism in those days was something new on the horizon. Mainly he was jumping to be on the wagon. I remember him in Cleveland, Ohio, in 1959, for example, during my ordination. In his speech during the banquet, he praised John XXIII. He praised him a lot. He said two voices were ringing in the ears of the world: the voice of John XXIII and the voice of Nikita Khrushchev. He made a comparison between Khrushchev and Pope John XXIII.

He was not an active ecumenist, I would say. But he had nothing against ecumenism. He thought it was a good movement, like Fr

George Florovsky, who in the beginning was very active in organizing the World Council of Churches. Later on George Florovsky lost interest. He felt that these people were not serious about the unity of the Church; they were busy preaching the social gospel only, helping churches here and there and so forth.

Did he believe the Church should take a stand on moral issues?

MP: Yes, he did. And from time to time we did help people in need. But he was busy doing his own work. As I said before, the archdiocese was a one-man organization, just Metropolitan Antony.

What was his attitude toward and his relationship with his second-generation laity in America?

MP: His relationship with the laity was, I would say, excellent. And we learned a great deal from him. As a matter of fact, when we study the history of our archdiocese, we find out that this archdiocese was not established by bishops or priests. It was established by the laypeople. When our people came to this country around the end of the nineteenth century and the beginning of the twentieth century, they were poor. They came here seeking freedom and economic opportunity, and so forth.

They were traveling from one place to another peddling their goods, their merchandise. They would arrive in Cedar Rapids, Iowa, for example, and feel exhausted. They couldn't walk any more in the cold in winter time and in the heat in summer time. So they would stay in Cedar Rapids, and their friends would follow them, and they would establish a community in Cedar Rapids. And they would pray in different homes as laypeople. That is what they did in Cedar Rapids, Iowa, in Omaha, Nebraska, in Beaumont, Texas, and so on in many of our traditional parishes in this archdiocese. These parishes were established by laypeople.

Then a missionary priest, a Syrian priest as they called him at the time, would travel from one city to another, conducting liturgies in the homes. He would pray for the dead; he would baptize the children; he would marry people at different homes until the community was strong enough to establish a church and get a priest, at first from St Raphael and later on, after 1936, from Metropolitan Antony.

Metropolitan Antony was very hesitant sometimes to . . . For example, Huntington, West Virginia—we have a thriving parish in Huntington, West Virginia. I told him one time we should establish a church in Huntington, West Virginia. He said, "No, these people cannot afford a church." He didn't want to. In Yonkers, I wanted to establish a parish when I was going to St Vladimir's Seminary. He did not like the idea at all. He said to me, "Don't waste your time; these people are busy in different restaurants making money. They're not thinking of the Church, so forget it." But I insisted, and we established a church in Yonkers, and the church in Yonkers is doing very well today. We have a very good community there.

Metropolitan Antony worked very well with the laity. He believed, as I believe today, that without the laypeople we will not have a Church in this country. They are the royal priesthood; the laypeople are the royal priesthood. They have a definite ministry to perform in the Church.

We have a problem in the old country because the laity are not involved in the life of the Church in the way they are involved in North America. Some of them are involved over there in Syria and Lebanon, but not to the extent that our laity are involved in the life of the Church in this country.

You know very well, as a priest in Oklahoma City, the contribution of the laity to your parish and to every parish. Without the laypeople, we would have no Church in North America. They are the foundation of the Church. We should encourage the laypeople instead of impose some kind of clericalism over them. We should let them work in the Church, but under the spiritual leadership of the priests. We should cultivate the talent that they have. We should cultivate these talents and use them for the glory of God.

Do you know anything about Antony's personal devotional life?

MP: Yes, I do. His personal devotional life was his work. This man was a man of unlimited energy. If you went to visit him during the day, forget it. He was working in his office upstairs in Bayridge in the house at 239 Eighty-Fifth Street. He would not receive anybody during the day at all. So he was completely devoted to the work of the archdiocese. He was not a man of contemplation. He was a man of action.

He was not a monk?

MP: No! Not by any means. He loved his cigars. He loved his big steaks. He loved his scotch. He was not a monk. No, no, he was not a monk.

He lived during the Great Depression, World War II, and the creation of the State of Israel. What effect did these events have on him? How did they shape his life?

MP: Well, let me tell you, you cannot separate the life of Metropolitan Antony from his era. He was born and grew up in a country that was part of the Ottoman Empire. And later on, it became a French mandate. Lebanon was a very poor country. He had an opportunity to study at the AUB, at the American University in Beirut, and learn English there and so forth. But the whole country was a poor country. There was poverty there. The Turks robbed the country, and then the French came and they discriminated against the Orthodox.

So when he came here, he came here against this background, a background of poverty. That's why money was so precious to him. You hear stories about his carefulness with money—I do not want to use another word—his carefulness with money. He was very careful with his money. He did not spend one penny, one single penny, foolishly. If he didn't want to spend, he wouldn't spend. If he didn't have to spend, he wouldn't spend on anything, on anyone at all.

I have so many stories to tell. Someday we will write a story about Metropolitan Antony and money and the humor of Metropolitan Antony. One time, Ilyas Kurban and I were in New York, and we decided to come and pay him a visit. We called and he said, "Well, I am busy during the day, you could come early in the morning and have breakfast with me." We went there to have breakfast. His sister, Adele, had one egg for me, one egg for Kurban, and one egg for Metropolitan Antony.

When we finished eating, he said, "Boys, remember the old radio?" They were big, bigger than the television today, a big radio. He had an old, big radio. He wanted us to take it to the third floor. Instead of hiring someone to take that big radio to the third floor, he asked Kurban and me to carry it up. I can't tell you how difficult it was taking that radio all the way to the third floor.

The idea of having breakfast with Metropolitan Antony was Kurban's idea. All the while we were dragging this thing upstairs to the third floor, I was screaming at Kurban quietly and telling him, "You wanted to have breakfast? Is this the kind of breakfast you wanted to have?" Anyhow, we have many, many, many stories like that about Metropolitan Antony.

And with the creation of the modern state of Israel?

MP: He was against that. Metropolitan Antony spoke against the establishment of the state of Israel at the expense of the Palestinian people. To him this was sheer injustice. He addressed that issue, but he was not a crusader. He was against the establishment. He thought that it did lots of injustice to the Palestinian people.

What kind of relationship did he have with heads of state, senators, congressmen, and other civil authorities? Did he seek to influence American foreign policy regarding the Middle East? Did he seek political assistance on behalf of the Christians in the Middle East?

MP: Well, I think he was perhaps the only archbishop who met with FDR at the White House. I am sure that, when he met with FDR, the Middle East was on the agenda of the meetings. So he tried in his own way and in his own limited times to influence politicians. Although he did not indulge very much in American politics. He would welcome and meet governors and mayors and so forth. But he was not that devoted to politics. He was busy organizing his archdiocese.

What was Antony's relationship with the other metropolitans of the Holy Synod of Antioch and with the late Patriarch?

MP: Sometimes good and sometimes tense. We have to remember that in 1936, when he was consecrated Metropolitan of New York and all

North America, at the same time, at the same hour, Archimandrite Samuel David was being consecrated as Archbishop of Toledo and Dependencies, again under the Syrian Archdiocese. So we had, in 1936, a very ugly situation here in America: two bishops over the same people and the same territories. We had to face the situation of two parishes in the same city, one belonging to New York [and one belonging to Toledo], like in Toledo, Ohio where you have St George and St Elias; you have in Boston, Massachusetts, St Mary's of Cambridge and St George and St John; you have in Wichita, Kansas, St Mary's and St George. In each of these cities, we had two Antiochian parishes under two different bishops.

This is a manifestation of the canonical chaos that persists in America until now, canonical chaos because our ancient canons prohibit the presence of more than one bishop over one city and one territory. Take New York City today. We have so many jurisdictions. You have Greek, you have OCA, you have Antiochian, you have Romanian, you have Serbian, you have Bulgarian. This is very much against the truth of Christ, against the spirit of the Orthodox Church.

The Church and nationalism do not coexist. We cannot say "the Russian Church," or the "Greek Church," or the "Arabic Church." But we can say the Church in Russia, the Church in Greece, the Church in Lebanon, and the Church in Syria. We cannot say the American Church, but we can say the Church in America, because Christ and His Church transcend nationalism and ethnicism.

Antony was consumed with trying to unite the Archdiocese with the late Archbishop Samuel David and the late Archbishop Michael Shaheen. In your understanding, why was unification not successful during his tenure?

MP: I remember, in 1973 I visited the late Archbishop Michael in Toledo, Ohio, and we started the process of reunification. I told him, "If we don't unite in this country, if we don't unite our people in the country, the Holy Synod of Antioch will never unite our people. We have to do it in this country."

If you read the minutes of the Holy Synod of Antioch from 1936 to 1970, you find the most contradictory decisions and the most shameful decisions. One year the Synod would decide in favor of New York; the next year, it would decide in favor of Toledo. You see and you hear fights. I remember when Bishop Antoun and I were deacons, subdeacons even, in St Elias Monastery during Synod meetings, we used to hear fights and screams.

So Antony did try. But he didn't go about it the right way. We have people from the Archdiocese of New York who perhaps did not encourage him enough, and the people of Toledo who really dictated to the late Samuel David. They didn't want him to have this unity.

And the way this unity happened was a gift, really. It was kind of a miracle after so many years. We had the schism of Russy-Antaky first, after the death of Hawaweeny. So for sixty years we knew nothing but division in this country, from 1915 to 1975; that's sixty years of division. Until in June 1975, Archbishop Michael and I met in Pittsburgh and put an end to this. Why did Metropolitan Antony fail? Well, he lived during different circumstances, and I don't want to say more than that.

As his successor, in what condition did you find the Archdiocese?

MP: The archdiocese had some sixty-five parishes, and we had a constitution that had to be updated completely; the parish constitutions and the archdiocese constitution were outdated. But we had lay organizations: SOYO was organized, and the board of trustees was organized, and parish councils were organized on the local level. Metropolitan Antony did lots of work. The first board of trustees was organized in 1948. Between 1936 and 1948, we did not have a board of trustees for parish dioceses.

After forty years in the episcopate yourself, you are in a unique position to evaluate Metropolitan Antony. From the vantage point of forty years down the road, how would you evaluate Antony's episcopacy?

MP: I believe that Antony's episcopacy was very successful for his particular era. He was the right man for that era. He served brilliantly from 1936 to 1966. Before he became archbishop, he was very fortunate to be a contemporary of great literary figures from the Middle East, people like Khalil Gibran, Makhael Neheme, Elia Abu Madi, Nadra Haddad and his brother, Abdul Nassir Haddad, the poet Nasib Areda of Humas, and Rashid Ayoub of Miskenta. He knew all these people. He socialized with them. He listened to their poetry. He was a literary figure himself. If you look at the issues of *The Word* magazine in English from 1957 to 1966, you will see his editorials are very fascinating. The man was a gifted man, and he did so much for this archdiocese. We are indebted to Metropolitan Antony Bashir.

What were Metropolitan Antony's strengths?

MP: His brilliance, his oratory gift, and his sense of humor. This man was really a master of the word. He knew how to express himself. When he delivered a speech, he could make you cry and he could make you laugh at the same time. He spoke in very, very penetrating words. He was a gifted, gifted speaker.

What were his weaknesses, if he had any?

MP: He lived with a sense of insecurity. For example, he never welcomed any bishop from the old country in this archdiocese. I remember when Archbishop Meletius Swaity returned from Latin America. You know he served in this archdiocese as a priest and then he was elected to be the vicar of the patriarch; I'm talking about Archbishop Meletius Swaity of thrice-blessed memory. He went to the old country, and he was serving in the Patriarchate as the patriarchal vicar. He had a problem with his eyes. So he returned to America to take care of his eyes in this country.

Metropolitan Antony had a fit, and he told him personally, "Why did you come back? Why are you coming back?" Swaity said, "Well, I came back to treat my eyes." And Antony said, "You have in the American University Hospital in Beirut the best eye doctors! You didn't have to come here!" So he had a sense of insecurity. Perhaps this sense of insecurity prevented him from having auxiliaries to assist him in the archdiocese.

Did not the Archdiocese Board of Trustees address this point once, and they agreed that they needed to have an assistant bishop to assist him, but it never materialized?

MP: Exactly! Exactly! This is the sense of insecurity that I am talking about. I mean, despite his greatness, despite the gifts that he had, still he had a sense of insecurity. He didn't want anyone to wear a crown in his own archdiocese. And he was very careful with his money, as I said. He was very frugal, is that the word?

Did he leave money to the Archdiocese, or did he spread it out?

MP: He promised to build the Balamand Theological School, St John of Damascus. He made this promise when he was in the old country. I was for this one hundred percent. As a matter of fact, we were coming together from the old country, and he was very, very unhappy about the trip, because the members of the Synod always gave him a rough time. Out of jealously. They were jealous of Metropolitan Antony. So he was sad on the plane, and I told him, "You know, Saidna, if you want really to help the Patriarchate of Antioch, and I know you love the Patriarchate of Antioch, if you want to help the Patriarchate, you must build a theological school for them." So that was the beginning of this venture. He paused for a while, and then he looked at me and said, "You know, you are right." He made a promise; he promised $250,000. Unfortunately, he died before he fulfilled his promise.

When I was elected, at the first meeting I attended of the Holy Synod of Antioch, I told them, "My predecessor made a promise to build a theological school, and I am going to fulfill his promise." On August 15, one day after my consecration, I traveled with the late Patriarch Theodosius Abourjaily, Theodosius VI of thrice-blessed memory, to the Balamand to break ground for the theological school. We did. My consecration was August 14. Then on August 15, 1966, we broke ground.

The school was dedicated in 1971. Our present patriarch, His Beatitude Ignatius IV Hazeem, was the dean of the Balamand at that particular time. So, I remember, I took a delegation with me in 1971, and we dedicated the new school.

So he left . . . Actually, I'm speaking now for history. The late Monsour Laham, the late Ted Makhoul, these people were my helps, my right arms, when I took over the archdiocese, for the financial matters. Perhaps Saidna Antoun remembers those days. We kept going from bank to bank to find the money in Brooklyn. Finally, I think we went to National City Bank where we found $600,000. That was all that Metropolitan Antony left. I repeat, $600,000. I did not touch that money. We kept the money. We invested the money. God rest his soul, Ted Makhoul did a great job helping us to invest the money. We established the Antony Bashir Memorial Fund. The money is still there; it's in the archdiocese. It is almost $3,000,000 now, if not more. I don't know exactly; I don't have the figures before me. But we did not spend the money.

Afterward, we established an annuity for his sister, Adele, because we didn't want to leave Adele penniless. Adele served this archdiocese. She was his cook, she was his secretary. She took books to the post office. She did everything for Metropolitan Antony. It was not fair just to leave her penniless. She had to leave the headquarters, you know, to live in her own place in Bayridge. But we created an annuity for her of, I believe, more than $200,000.

After I become successor to Metropolitan Antony, I always paid her visits. And so did (at the time Father, and now Bishop) Antoun Khoury, after he came back to help me. He was in Toronto, you know. I asked him to come and help me in Bayridge. I don't think I did him a big favor, but history will tell.

When Metropolitan Antony passed away, you were chosen to give the eulogy at his funeral. How were you chosen to do that? Who asked you?

MP: That's a very, very interesting question. I never thought about it. I always wrote good Arabic. I still write good Arabic. The late Protosyngellos Ellis Khoury loved the Arabic language. He was a good writer and good speaker himself. May his soul rest in peace. He was a great man. I will always cherish his friendship. He was a good helper; as protosyngellos he did an excellent job. So he and the priests that knew me well in the archdiocese chose me because I knew Arabic very well and my English wasn't bad. They just asked me. I was surprised when they asked me to give the eulogy. So I spoke on behalf of the clergy, in both languages, Arabic and English. In fact, I composed a short poem at that time. So it was the wish of Fr Ellis Khoury and the clergy in those days that I eulogize, that I speak on behalf of the clergy. And I did.

You mentioned that you were on an airplane coming back from Lebanon. Was this a special trip that you both went on, a special occasion, or just a coincidence that you were on the same airplane?

MP: It was 1961. We went there to attend the Holy Synod meeting, because at that meeting Fr Ilyas Kurban, who was the pastor of St George parish of Boston, Massachusetts, was elected metropolitan of the Archdiocese of Tripoli, El Koura and Dependencies. After some tension in that archdiocese between two clergymen who wanted to be the metropolitan, Kurban was elected to solve the problem. At the same time, Archimandrite Michael Shaheen was elected bishop to help Metropolitan Antony.

When I came back to Cleveland, Fr Kurban called me and said, "What did you do there?" I replied, "We elected you Metropolitan of Tripoli." He said, "You think you did me a favor?" I remember that.

The second thing I remember is that Bishop Shaheen came back, and Metropolitan Antony put him in Montreal at St George Parish. He was the pastor of that parish. He came back and put him in Montreal, instead of asking Shaheen to assist him and visit, make visitations to parishes here and there. The problem of Toledo and New York could have been solved at that time.

Unfortunately, these are the accidents of history. Unfortunately, Metropolitan Antony left Archbishop Michael in Montreal to serve as a priest without asking him to do anything in the archdiocese. That's what tempted the late Archbishop Michael to accept the offer of the Toledo group to leave Montreal and come to Toledo and become the Archbishop of Toledo. So the schism persisted. The Toledo-New York schism persisted. It could have ended in 1962, but it did not, unfortunately. These are two significant events.

What stories, incidents, or recollections stand out in what you know or heard about Antony?

MP: Metropolitan Antony was a very wise man. He learned from his own life experience, which was very rich. He came from the old country to this country during, as I said before, a very difficult time. He lived through the Depression years. Many people in this country lost their fortunes, and some of them even committed suicide during the Depression. So that is the only way I can explain his carefulness with money.

Beside that, the man had a very, very outstanding sense of humor. I remember one time he told me this story: He had a priest that was not able to remain in the same parish for more than six months or a year. Then he would have a fight with his parishioners and leave the parish and come to the bishop and ask for another parish. That happened so many times that the bishop got fed up. So one day, as the Metropolitan was working in his little office in Bayridge, this priest came again and told him, "Saidna, I am very tired of that parish." The Metropolitan said, "You have been tired of so many parishes! Let me see what I can do for you. You want to leave the parish now?" "Well, I want a peaceful parish," the priest said. So he wrote an address for him. He gave this address to him. He said, "Here in Brooklyn we have a very peaceful parish."

The priest was excited. He got the address from the archbishop, and went to the street and grabbed a cab. He gave the taxicab driver the address and said, "Please take me to this address." The taxicab took him all the way to Greenwood Cemetery. The driver said, "This is the address that you gave me; look at it, look at it on the wall." The priest looked and he saw a cemetery. There was no church. He was furious.

He went back to the archbishop and said to him, "Saidna, you gave me this address. This is the address of a cemetery." The archbishop replied, "Well, you wanted a peaceful parish. Only dead people are peaceful people!"

Another time, he was visiting a parish that had built a new church. The wealthiest man in the parish took the archbishop to show him the church. As they walked in, the wealthy man started criticizing the icons. He said to the archbishop, "I don't like these icons; we need different icons, better icons. I don't like the windows; they did not do them right. I don't like the Pantokrator; they didn't do that right. I don't like the pews."

He kept complaining and complaining. Finally Metropolitan Antony said, "Well, okay, we are going to change the icons; we are going to change the windows; we will change the pews; we will change everything that you don't like here. But how much money are you going to contribute?" This man had never contributed a penny to the parish in his life. The guy said, "I'm not here to tell you how much money I'm going to contribute. I am here to give you opinions." He was going to contribute his opinions. The metropolitan got very upset with him and said to him, "You give me opinions? I'm giving opinions to the whole world. I don't need your opinions. Let's go!"

Once, when he came to Cleveland, Ohio, I told him that Mr So-and-so was in the hospital and asked if he would to go and say a prayer for him. He said, "Sure!" We went to the hospital. As we were walking in the hospital, unexpectedly he stepped on my foot. He was a big man. I said, "Awwww!": He said, "What's the matter with you?" I said, "You stepped on my foot." He said, "That's okay; it could have been worse." I said, "What's worse than that?" He said, "Had you stepped on mine."

He was very private. How many close friends did he have?

MP: Not many. I think his best friend was the poet Elia Abu Madi. They lived next door to each other. They used to play cards every night. He loved this game called trump or whist. He played whist with Elia Abu Madi and some old-timers from Brooklyn almost every night.

Your Eminence, if you will permit me a personal question: When my father came from the old country, how was my father convinced to stay? How did he reach Metropolitan Antony Bashir, and how was it that you came to shave my father's beard?

MP: Your dad came after the war of 1948 in Palestine. After the partitioning of Palestine, he came to this country. That was a very sad time in Palestine. He came here, trying to collect some money, I guess, for orphanages there or for a school. I don't know how much he needed. I was not privy to that.

But I had a few talks with your dad. I told him, "There is no future for you in Palestine right now. That society is upside down. It is a troubled society. Why don't you stay here in America?"

So I asked Metropolitan Antony a few times, "This man is a family man, a good man. He is not lazy. He is a good worker." Metropolitan Antony was very reluctant to accept priests, especially from the old country. Finally he acquiesced. He said, "Okay, but you must shave his beard."

Your dad had a thick, long, black beard. He was young. He came to Detroit, and I was going to Wayne State University in those days. I said, "Abouna Zachariah, we're going to shave your beard." He said, "What?" I said, "We're going to shave your beard. If you want to stay in this country, you have to get rid of this beard. You saw the priests in America; they don't have beards like that."

He said to me, "But I have had this beard for a long time." I said, "Well, you have to choose between your beard and this country." He said, "Okay, why don't you shave my beard?" So I got my scissors and my razor, and I started working. When I shaved his beard, and he looked at the mirror, he started crying. He cried. He said to me, "I don't look the same." And I replied, "I know you don't look the same."

Your Eminence, thank you for giving of your time and for sharing your reflections on your predecessor, Metropolitan Bashir. May God grant you many years.

CHAPTER 14

A Private Look

It is important to remember that, before anything else, Antony Bashir was a man. He was capable of compassion and kindness, but he was also capable of sternness and stinginess. It is impossible to overstate the debt owed to this founding father of the Antiochian Archdiocese, but the greatness of what he achieved should not be permitted to obscure his humanity.

Antony was a listener and observer. He cherished receiving recommendations and speaking in a practical manner on every level. He utilized young and talented parishioners and constantly sought for the mission of the church financially, even if it was necessary for him to "ride a donkey"[1] to get to his destination. He showed his love and concern toward the youth, encouraging the young men to produce documents to guide and address the newly established SOYO of the Eastern Region.[2] He wanted the young men and women to meet at the conventions and have debutante balls.

In order to better provide a private look at Antony, I am including some personal stories that various people remember and tell about him.

Daniel Kasis Remembers Bashir

My grandfather, Abraham Kasis, was one of the founders of St George Cathedral in Charleston, West Virginia. Antony Bashir, when he was

---

[1]From a personal interview with Daniel Kasis, held on May 26, 2007 in Toledo, OH.

[2]From a personal interview with George Nassar, held on July 23, 2007 in Montreal, Canada.

a priest, stayed at my grandfather's home. On one occasion, they were on their way to church. It was a very bad day. It was raining. The streets at that time weren't paved, and cars were just beginning to be seen. This was in the 1920s.

My grandfather had a donkey, a jackass, and he told the priest, "I don't want you to get your feet wet or muddy. You ride on the donkey." Antony Bashir replied, "There's no way I'm going to get on this donkey, no way."

My grandfather was a very strong, forceful man. He stuck his fingers out, pointing at Bashir, and said, "Are you better than Jesus Christ?"

Antony thought about it, relented, and got on the donkey, and they went to church.[3]

George Nasser Remembers Bashir

Eddie Deeb, the first president of the Eastern Region SOYO, asked me recently if I remembered when Saidna Antony locked us in the boiler room at the cathedral in Brooklyn and told us we were not getting out until we finished the constitution for the Eastern Region SOYO. Of course I remember. There was a group of representatives from St George Church in Patterson and from the cathedral, to form the Eastern Region SOYO at the request of Saidna.

Another time, as a youngster, I remember working with my father after school. Saidna drove down from New England in a new Chevy that he had been given up there. He yelled at my father, "I need new fixtures for my house in Brooklyn." And I carried those fixtures out and put them in his car. And God rest his soul, when we visited his home after his passing, I went into his house and I recognized the fixtures that were still in the house that I, as a little boy, had put in his car.[4]

---

[3]Kasis, personal interview.

[4]From a personal interview with George Nassar, held on July 23, 2007 in Montreal, Canada.

Bishop Antoun Khouri Will Never Forget Antony Bashir

I was in Brazil. Fr George Rados was there. He said, "Why don't you come to America? It is much better. Fr Schmemann and others like him are now teaching there." So we talked with my metropolitan, and he wrote to Metropolitan Antony Bashir to ask him how much would it cost for me to go there. God bless him. I applied. I had two gentlemen who were here at that time, Philip Saliba and Emile Hanna, retired now. Both of them were working for me to come to the United States. When I got the okay from my metropolitan, Metropolitan Bashir then said okay. My metropolitan wrote a letter, and Metropolitan Antony accepted me. And I came.

Metropolitan Antony sent a priest to meet me at the airport. Fr Joachim Dalack picked me up and took me to his home for the night. The next day he took me to the seminary. After a few days, Fr Joachim Dalack took me to meet Metropolitan Antony Bashir. I had met him once before in Damascus. He was a tall, handsome man, with authority. We liked his philosophy about life. We had read about him and what he had done in America.

He welcomed me and gave me some work to do in the yard. That was my first impression: he put you to work right away. Then, when I had some problem with my metropolitan in Brazil, he called me in with Fr Joseph Shaheen. Fr Shaheen picked me up from the seminary, because we were still in school. He took me to Metropolitan Antony. The Metropolitan said to me, "Why don't you stay here?" "I don't know if my bishop will give me permission," I replied. "Don't worry about it," he said. He wrote my metropolitan. He called me and told me he had received a letter from my metropolitan giving me the freedom to go any place to school. He asked me, because I'd had bad experiences with bishops, if I'd like to stay here and go to school.

But I didn't want to be ordained a priest at that time until I had finished school. Metropolitan Philip Saliba, who was a priest at that time, encouraged me and said, "If Metropolitan Antony told you he's going to do something, he will do it. Just accept it." Metropolitan Antony said to me, "I have a proposal for you. I'm going to have you be ordained a priest so you can help us during the summer time." He ordained me in Boston at the New England Parish Life Conference on May 29, 1960. It was Memorial Day weekend. Of course, I didn't know then that it was called Memorial Day weekend. But it was Memorial Day weekend, 1960.

He liked the way I conducted the services. One time, after I was ordained a priest, we were at a convention, I think the Eastern Region Parish Life Conference in Miami, Florida. He looked at the priests and told them, "This baby priest"—I was the youngest ordained that year—"what he does in the vespers and the liturgies, watch him. He's the best teacher there can be." I was really very nervous among all the priests after that.

Everyone knew how tight Metropolitan Antony was with money. However, he was very kind to me. As a seminarian he gave me a scholarship. He also gave me $100 a month—to rent a room for $25 and $75 to eat and live on. He paid for the second and third year of seminary after he appointed me to go to Philadelphia, which meant I was traveling between Philadelphia and New York City (at that time St Vladimir's Seminary was at 121st Street and Broadway in New York).

I never celebrate the Divine Liturgy without mentioning Metropolitan Antony, because had he not helped me at that time, I don't know where I would be today. I will never forget Metropolitan Antony as long as I live.[5]

Dr John Dalack's Private Look at Antony Bashir

I lived not very far from Metropolitan Antony. My father was dean of the cathedral from 1948 to 1962. There were many ways that I saw Metropolitan Antony officially and informally. The archbishop was in the habit of calling the two priests that lived near him. Fr Paul Schneirla was the pastor of St Mary's, which was on Eighty-first Street; the Archdiocese headquarters was on Eighty-Fifth. My father lived on Ninety-second Street, and even though the Cathedral was downtown, we were very close to him.

[5]From a personal interview with Bishop Antoun Khouri, held on July 24, 2007 in Montreal, Canada.

Very often, when the archbishop needed something, he would call either my father or Fr Paul. On one occasion, the archbishop called Fr Paul Schneirla and asked him to come to the Archdiocese office on Eighty-Fifth Street. Fr Paul said, "Saidna, I'm not feeling well. I'm quite sick." "What's wrong?" Antony asked.

Well, Fr Paul Schneirla loved to eat. Someone had given him six bowls of *shangleesh*, which is a kind of cottage cheese that has turned. It's very tasty. Fr Paul had eaten all six bowls. And the archbishop said, "Fr Paul, anyone who eats six bowls of *shangleesh* deserves to be sick!"

The archbishop was in the habit of taking care of all his correspondence and mail personally. There was no secretary. He lived in the house on Eighty-Fifth Street basically alone. But he had his sister, Adele, whom we always referred to as Aunt Adele. And she did help him in many ways. But she was not a secretary. Metropolitan Antony was in the habit, when he received a letter . . . his typical plan was, to turn the letter over and write his answer to the letter on the back. He would then put books or whatever packages he had with it and carry them himself. His house was on Eighty-Fifth Street between Second and Third Avenue. The Post Office was on Eighty-Sixth Street and Fifth Avenue. He would walk. All the kids would see him in his black Stetson hat. He was a very tall, distinguished man.

He walked carrying his packages. If any of us were around, of course we would run and help him carry things. But that was his thing. He was very, very efficient and very self-sufficient.

When my father was ordained to the priesthood in 1948, the home that we were going to move into in Brooklyn was not ready yet. And so he invited us to live at the archdiocese—my mother, my father, my brother and I—to live in the archdiocese. It was maybe two and a half to three months that we lived there. So we had a chance to see him in a very informal way. My brother and I went to a boarding school at the time when my father was ordained in 1948. But on weekends and holidays we were home, while we were living in the archdiocese.

He loved to smoke his cigars. He smoked only La Corona Coronas, which in those days were an expensive cigar. He liked a quiet evening at home, either playing whist in his house or playing whist next door. He lived next door to Elia Abu Madi, who was a very famous Arabic poet. I grew up with Elia's son, Robert, and we were close friends. And so we would see Antony playing whist with Elias, with my father, and with various visiting dignitaries, either at the archdiocese headquarters or the Abu Madi home.

Metropolitan Antony did not like to lose at whist. He was not a cheerful loser. He loved to win, and he loved to gloat when he won. When things did not go well because of someone's misplay, he was not very happy about that. It was like a family to see the way he reacted when things did not go well.

On one occasion, when I was living at the archdiocese, Metropolitan Antony had to make a trip. And the weather was still cold. My father was ordained in February, so it was still cold in February and March. He told us he wanted us to start up the engine on his Cadillac, so that the battery wouldn't go dead. I was fourteen or fifteen years old at the time, so I didn't have a license. But my brother had a license, and he decided he would be the one, obviously, to start the car and run the engine a little bit. And he figured as long as we're running the engine, we might as well use the car. He got in the habit of driving around, running local errands and things like that. You can see the headlines, "Priest's kids hijack the metropolitan's Cadillac." We didn't go far. We made a few short trips, all in the name of honoring the bishop's request that we run the car.

Metropolitan Antony used to serve many divine liturgies in St Nicholas Cathedral. I was an altar boy. He was not hard to serve with at all, but there are a few stories I will tell you.

When the metropolitan became impatient and wanted things to go more quickly, there were occasions when he turned two or three pages at a time, and the priests had trouble following where he was because he would skip ahead. He also enjoyed giving sermons. Fr Paul and my father encouraged him to give his sermon right after the gospel. He seldom did that. What he preferred to do was to wait until the end of the service. After he had his communion and had communed the priests, while the priests distributed communion to the people, Metropolitan Antony would sit down, and we altar boys would bring him a goblet of wine and a half a loaf of bread. He would drink that, and then he'd get up to speak. He had not eaten the bread but he had drunk the wine, and there were occasions when he said various funny things. For example, one that stands out in my mind: he was going on about whatever the gospel happened to be at that time, and he ended by saying, "As God said in two words, 'Love thy neighbor.' "

One time, as he was giving his sermon, he looked out into the congregation and saw somebody chewing gum. He said, "I don't want you to chew gum. I want you to get rid of the gum." People swallowed their gum right on the spot. He was a strict disciplinarian.

Metropolitan Antony was a very innovative man in many ways. He's the one who began the whole process of having things done in English. He also was very instrumental in getting our boys in the seminaries. And he also was very eager to get SOYO started. What he told me at one point was this: "You know, our boys go to these meetings [a thing in those days called The Federation], our boys go, and they meet girls from other religions, and they end up getting married. And I don't like that. We've got to start something within our Archdiocese so that Orthodox boys and girls can meet each other."

There's an old expression that, to me, sums up what Metropolitan Antony meant and still means to this archdiocese. He is the one who put us on his shoulders, so to speak, and once we were on his shoulders, there was a lot we could see and do. He put us in a position that we could achieve what has been achieved. By putting us on his shoulders, we were able to see much more than he could see. He was the person we needed for the time. What he was able to do for the Church needed to be done. He was as important in his day as any of the current issues are in our day.

Everything we have, organizationally, started from him. In those days, there was very little for choirs, very little for church schools. The work he started initially was SOYO. SOYO was the church school and SOYO was the choir. Over the years they became independent and separate departments. And of course, today under Metropolitan Philip, we have created other organizations such as the Antiochian Women and the Order of St Ignatius. But the springboard from which everything came was SOYO. It was kind of Metropolitan Antony's baby.[6]

Bob Laham on Reunification Efforts

Metropolitan Antony and my dad were extremely close. Every time Metropolitan Antony came to Boston, he used to room with us; he used to come to our home. Contrary to his very stern appearance, he was an extremely mild and generous person. He knew that he was always called a penny-pincher and a money grabber, but he was quite the contrary. He would have given you anything off his back.

He was in Boston when he passed away. I was with him. My dad and I went to be in his room the night he passed away. In the three or four days he was in Boston, those final days, he gave my dad all the information about where everything was. He wanted to make sure everything was passed on to the archdiocese. He didn't even leave a penny to his family. The board of trustees decided there should be a bit of money given to his sister, Adele. She was the one who had taken care of him all the years.

Metropolitan Antony typed everything himself. He was a one-finger typer. He wasn't a very good typist. It is amazing the work he did and was able to do.

In 1955, there was an attempt at reconciliation with Toledo. I was at the meeting with Anna Douad and with Mary Douad, who was the powerhouse of the Toledo Diocese. Metropolitan Antony and my dad and I drove down and visited with Metropolitan Samuel David. And we pounded out an agreement in 1955. It was in the afternoon, and Mary said to my dad that Metropolitan Antony would never, never sign the agreement. Immediately, my dad had me call Metropolitan Antony, who was in his room on the top floor. It was the Sheraton Country Plaza at the time in Boston. Metropolitan Antony came down to Metropolitan Samuel David's suite. My dad handed him the agreement. Metropolitan Antony said, "Monsour, do you agree with this agreement?" My dad said, "Yes." He took out his pen and signed it.

[6]From a personal interview with Dr John Dalack, held July 25, 2007 in Montreal, Canada.

We had an agreement in principle. We meant for both dioceses to be together. They were very happy about it. Metropolitans Antony and Samuel were not controversial with each other. It was always the ladies that were the problem. We all went upstairs and went to bed. We thought everything was set. They next morning Mary calls up, "Nope, there's something wrong." She was a very powerful person. She ruined the whole thing. It was amazing. Metropolitans Antony and David really wanted to make it work, but they just couldn't accomplish it because of the ladies.

I was there before Archbishop Michael became an archbishop. He came to Boston and met with Metropolitan Antony, my dad, and myself at the Red Coach Inn on Standhope Street. He swore allegiance to Metropolitan Antony, that he would never do anything to upset the apple cart of the North American archdiocese and would always be subject to it. However, when they went overseas, Mary insisted they would not accept him unless he became a metropolitan, and he conceded and became one. But it was always an amicable situation between Archbishop Antony and Archbishop Michael.[7]

Philip Haddad Reflects on the Old Days

I knew Archbishop Antony Bashir during the administration of Metropolitan Samuel David. Antony was a dear friend of mine. I knew him quite well, because I had a cousin of mine, Fr Emile Hanna, who was with him. At that time, I did not know Metropolitan Philip, who was in the seminary in Lebanon with Fr Emile.

Once, when Bishop Samuel David was in Charleston, he asked me to do him a favor. I said, "What is it?" He said, "Fr Emile would like to come to the United States and become a priest in our diocese." So naturally, we took care of the arrangements. Two weeks later, Metropolitan David called me and said, "Emile does not want to come. He's decided to change his mind because Philip Saliba was not invited to come, and he won't come unless he comes." So we had to work things out for him, and they both came over at that time from Lebanon.

---

[7]Bob Laham, personal interview.

Later, when Emile was being ordained to the priesthood in Ottawa, Canada, we went to the ordination, and we enjoyed it. Metropolitan Antony sat next to me; I sat next to him, rather. We talked and discussed the program. He said, "I want to thank you for what you did." He and I were good friends. We would tell each other jokes. He was a great man. We were a little concerned about him at the time, about his health. I asked him, "Do you have a successor?" He said, "Well, not at the present time." I told him, "Well, Saidna, you should have someone to assist you. And if anything does happen, you've got someone to replace you and take over." Of course, none of us knew then that Philip Saliba, who had come here with Emile Hanna, would one day be chosen to take Metropolitan Antony's place upon his passing.

I want to tell you a story about Samuel David and Antony Bashir. We had a meeting of the diocese either in Chicago or Detroit, I don't remember which. I went with my uncle and father-in-law. At one point, I said, "We're going to have a party." So we went to get some food and drink. When we came back, we heard someone from a room on our same floor playing the *oud*. We gathered around the door listening. When it opened, inside were Antony and Samuel David singing together. They really did get along.[8]

Fr George Rados' Anecdotes

As a seminarian at the Greek Orthodox seminary in Brookline, Massachusetts, I had the opportunity to sit close to His Eminence Metropolitan Antony Bashir at a banquet held at St George's Church, when it was located on St James Street in Boston. Needless to say, I was enamored with the archbishop from my youth up because of his great presence and ability to impress everyone with his keen wit, wisdom, and humor. His command of conversation was such that one was spellbound by his stories, and one simply listened without interrupting.

On this occasion, an elderly man approached Saidna Antony at the head table and offered him a thin inexpensive cigar to enjoy smoking

[8]From a personal interview with Philip Haddad, held July 25, 2007 in Montreal, Canada.

after dinner. In those days it probably did not cost more than five or ten cents. This was a sure sign that the old man did not know the archbishop very well, because Saidna only smoked Havana cigars that came in individually wrapped tubes costing approximately three dollars or so. Neither did the old man know that the metropolitan was a very frugal man.

"Here, Saidna, is a cigar to enjoy after dinner," said the old man. The archbishop looked up and, trying to be appreciative, said, "Thank you, ya ummie [Uncle], but I do not smoke this kind of cigar because it is too strong for me." The elder was taken aback a bit at the refusal and thought it would be a good comeback if he asked for one of the archbishop's cigars. "No, ya ummie, mine are too mild for you."[9]

It was September 1954 when seven young men came together as seminarians at Holy Cross Greek Orthodox Seminary in Brookline, Massachusetts. The seminary had just received accreditation from this New England state to issue a Bachelor of Arts degree as well as a Masters in Theology. This was the incentive that convinced Archbishop Bashir to gather together his seminarians, who were scattered throughout various universities. The seminarians were: Michael Azkoul of Grand Rapids, Michigan; George S. Corey of Charleston, West Virginia; Louis Mashie of Syracuse, New York; Ray Ofiesh of New Kensington, Pennsylvania; Fr Tom Ruffin of Cedar Rapids, Iowa (already an assistant pastor at St George of Worchester, Massachusetts); and George Rados and Fred Shaheen, both of Canton, Ohio.

After coming together for the first time, it was not long before a bond of brotherhood grew among these seminarians. They were the pride and joy of Metropolitan Antony, for they represented a new era of well-trained theologians. They created a pattern for future young men who would excel beyond description.

This introduction to the anecdote was necessary to describe two events in particular relating to the unique personality of Antony Bashir. While studying at Holy Cross in Boston, we were visited by the Metropolitan of Toledo and Dependencies, Samuel David. He invited

[9]Personal comments received from Fr George Rados by email, July 30, 2007.

ANTONY BASHIR: METROPOLITAN & MISSIONARY

us to have dinner with him at the Nile Restaurant. We had the blue plate special (a combination of Arabic food) that we all savored; this food was missed in the seminary's cuisine. Following the dinner, the archbishop told us that we were also his seminarians in addition to being Bashir's. He proceeded to open his napkin on the cleared table. He then laid seven gold-chained crosses on the napkin, alongside seven framed pictures of himself. After blessing the crosses and chanting the *troparion* of the Holy Cross, he invited each of us to come forward to receive his blessing by hanging the crosses around our necks and receiving his picture. Needless to say, we were overcome with appreciation and with an unforgettable memory.

Shortly after this event, several of us drove to New York on our way home for Christmas. We called Metropolitan Antony and asked if we could visit him before separating to journey to our respective homes. We were welcomed at the archdiocese by His Eminence, his sister Adele, and Deacon Ilyas Kurban, a recent arrival from Lebanon. We were decked out with our black suits and ties and proudly displayed our crosses on our chests.

"Well, boys, how are you, and how are you doing in your studies?" asked Saidna. We all answered, "Well." "By the way, Saidna, we were recently visited by Metropolitan Samuel David, and he gave us the crosses we are wearing along with a framed picture of himself," said one of the boys.

After a nice conversation, Saidna Antony excused himself before we left and reappeared a few minutes later telling us that here were some gifts from "your own archbishop." We departed from the archdiocese with a can of pistachios and a larger unframed picture of himself.

The second part of this anecdote is similar to the first. Saidna Antony moved his seminarians from Holy Cross to St Vladimir's, so that we could continue our classes in English, for the new dean at Holy Cross, Bishop Athenagoras, insisted on us taking all our classes and writing all our papers in Greek when we returned for our third year of studies. We now found ourselves at 212th Street and Broadway in New York City. The seminary was housed in an apartment building across from Union Theological Seminary and next to Columbia University. This move brought us closer to the archdiocese in Brooklyn. We were called upon from time to time to go to Saidna's home to work on repairs and prepare for seasonal changes such as hanging storm windows in the winter or screens for the summer.

The metropolitan called us to his residence one day for a nice chat. He told us that he had some new raincoats that he wanted to give each of us, for helping around the house. We were all excited, thinking that we were about to get a new London Fog raincoat. We were sitting on pins and needles during our conversation with him, when he finally said, "Boys, go out on the porch and open those large boxes and take out a coat of your size." We left that day clad in a rubber fireman's coat with metal clasps. Somehow our fire was suddenly extinguished.[10]

The first group of seminarians graduated from St Vladimir's Seminary in 1958. The ceremonies took place in St Mary's Antiochian Orthodox Church in Brooklyn, New York. Metropolitan Antony Bashir was the guest speaker. His remarks concentrated on the good advice a father would give to his sons as they were about to begin their careers in life. He began by saying that we were now graduating from the "school of books," but that we had to go through another school from which we may never graduate, and that was the "school of life."

He told us, "When you go to your parishes, don't try to stuff Jesus Christ down the throats of your parishioners. He waited 2,000 years, and a few more years won't hurt." At this point in his remarks, the seminary professors, sitting on the edge of their seats, were waiting to hear what justification the archbishop would give for making such a statement. "Endear yourself first to your parishioners," he continued. "When they love and respect you as their spiritual father, they will accept Christ in any way, shape, or form you offer him to them. Be like a heavy-laden fruit tree whose bended limbs offer its fruit for easy picking. Be humble, kind, and loving."

Well, there was a great sigh of relief, and the professors sat back in their seats waiting for what was to come next.

"Now, when you come across a 'hardhead,' don't just walk away from him; manipulate him, calm him, compliment him, and allay his

[10]Ibid., August 2, 2007.

complaints by massaging his better side. If you ever want to avoid getting caught in the claws of a lobster, all you have to do is turn him over and massage his underbelly until those claws submissively open and render him helpless. Then and only then will he turn red with embarrassment for the trouble he's caused you."

There were no theological statements, no saintly quotations, only the wisdom of a man you could not help but love. Such advice I cherished and made my priestly rule.[11]

During the reign of Metropolitan Antony Bashir, the Greek Orthodox Archdiocese in the United States was headed by the noted Archbishop Athenagoras, who eventually became Patriarch of Constantinople. They were close friends during their mutual years of ruling their respective archdioceses.

Apparently, the Greek Archdiocese was experiencing a lack of administrative leadership, while the Syrian Archdiocese was prospering in growth and influence. Once, when the archbishops were together, Archbishop Athenagoras asked Archbishop Antony what he was doing to advance the success of his Archdiocese.

"Give more responsibility to the youth of the church. Let them take over organizing religious education, music, regional youth chapters, and the like. Help them identify with their ethnic background: food, dance, language, and heritage."

This was his advice to Archbishop Athenagoras. Archbishop Athenagoras heeded Anthony's advice and created GOYA (Greek Orthodox Youth of America), that mirrored our own SOYO (Syrian Orthodox Youth Organization). SOYO became the network that united the Syrian Orthodox Archdiocese of North America. Annual regional conventions were sponsored to organize Sunday schools, choirs, and local chapters for the purpose of encouraging Orthodox acquaintances. Such events and programs resulted in many marriages and lifetime distant relationships, as well as the use of the English language, melodious choirs, and religious education. Metropolitan Antony practiced what he preached. Such was the advice of Saidna Antony to Theofilestatos Athenagoras.[12]

[11]Ibid., August 13, 2007.
[12]Ibid., August 30, 2007.

A Private Look

William F. Bitar Remembers Metropolitan Antony

In 1958, my father Frank and I were in Utah, attempting to discover a much wanted mineral at that time in great demand—uranium. After we had been there for a while, we drove to Los Angeles to attend the archdiocese convention where my mother, Margaret, coming from Portland, was to meet us and enjoy the festivities. At the conclusion of the Divine Liturgy, the Metropolitan was about to process out down the center aisle with his crown on and candles in both hands. He proceeded down the aisle, and as he did so, he said, "Remember there are still tickets available for the grand banquet." In other words, His Eminence was selling even on the way out.

In the summer of 1959, I was asked to attend the archdiocese convention in Toledo, Ohio, as the representative from St George Church in Portland, Oregon, because our parish priest was being reassigned to another parish. It was a great experience for me to be able to attend the convention for the first time in the eastern part of the United States. At the conclusion of one evening's events, the metropolitan came to the podium and asked all the unmarried girls to come forward. We soon discovered that His Eminence was attempting to get his seminarians married so he could ordain them to the priesthood. "Girls," he said, "come up here, for I have some seminarians who want to *mazweg* ('get married' in Arabic)!"

He was a most unforgettable and loving man. I also remember vividly the 1960 convention in Houston, Texas. We were all seated for the grand banquet in the prestigious Shamrock Hilton. All of a sudden, the banquet door opened and in came His Eminence, in full dress, with his staff in hand, followed by all his priests and the entourage that normally accompanied him for his grand entrance. As he entered the room, he stopped, surveyed the whole room, and noticed that everyone was still seated but clapping to greet him. Pausing, he said in a deep voice, loud and full of gusto, "Stand up!" He motioned as he said it; and I imagined he was probably saying to himself, "Show me some proper respect. Don't you know who I am? The proper thing to do is to stand up!"

He was indeed a great leader of our Church, and because of his fine leadership and example to us, the Church grew rapidly in those early years as it established itself in America. He was ahead of his time as he led the Church in America. The translation of the liturgy into English came early on because of his far-sightedness.[13]

Reminiscences of Father Joseph Shaheen

He had physical stature. It was my job to carry his mantya because I was also tall. He was a man of magnificent character. At a convention, he would invite some priests to come to his room. Once there, he would ask them if they had any jokes or stories to tell. We would share some with him. During the convention he would change the joke, modify it, and manipulate it in order to achieve the desired purpose when he told it.

He used to say, "I may be a bishop, but you are my hands. I may be a bishop, but you are my feet. I may be a bishop, but you are my voice."

Even though Bashir was, in many ways, a loner who did everything himself, these comments let us know that he knew the archdiocese was not a one-man show. He knew that he and the clergy, he and the board, and he and the laity, had a synergistic relationship. They needed a bishop to lead them, but he needed them to follow him.

Archpriest Tom Ruffin was very close to Bashir. At the conventions, he always invited Fr Tom to his room. At one convention, he was in Ruffin's room and decided to make a phone call to Archbishop Iakovos. He picked up the phone and got the operator. He told her who he was and that he wanted to make a call and have it charged to his room. The operator had him spell his name. "B-A-S-H-I-R." "No, no," he said, and spelled it again. And then he spelled his name yet again for a third time. Then the operator had him spell Ruffin. "R-U-F-F-I-N." Again, it took three or four times before she got it right. Then he told her he wanted to call Archbishop Iakovos. Once again the operator asked him to spell Iakovos. In his deep voice, and totally

---

[13]From personal comments from William F. Bitar.

---

exasperated, Bashir replied, "For God's sake, if you can't get the spelling of Bashir, and you can't get the spelling of Ruffin, you'll never get Iakovos!" And he hung up the phone.

Antony Bashir believed a man should be in charge of his life. He could not control the incompetence of the operator, but he could control how long he would waste trying to accomplish a task with her.

After Antony Bashir died, Archpriest James Meena had a photo of Bashir printed with a quotation from Bashir as a caption, "No one can divide you unless you want to." Even in death, his words reminded his flock that they were not at the mercy of others. They were responsible for what they did with their lives and, collectively, what they did with the archdiocese.[14]

Reminiscences of Father John Badeen

Bashir arrived at either Detroit or Toledo for a convention. He was received by the mayor, the police commissioner, and other city officials, along with many parishioners. He was treated royally. Some went to get his luggage. Others greeted him with flowers. The police escorted his motorcade to the hotel. That evening he told some friends that he felt like he was ten feet tall. On Sunday morning, he vested and entered the church in procession where he was greeted with applause and best wishes. In the evening he repeated himself, "I've never felt this way. I feel like I am ten feet tall."

When the convention was over, Antony returned home to New York. There was no one to greet him at the station. He retrieved his own suitcase and carried it outside where he waved down a taxi, got in, and told the driver to take him to Brooklyn. The driver stopped, told him he didn't go to Brooklyn, and let Bashir out. At that moment he said he felt about five feet tall.

He got another taxi and arrived at home. He carried his suitcase up the steps, opened the door, and went in. His sister Adele said, "Antony, will you come here and pick up the garbage and carry it outside." He now felt two feet tall. "And then the reality hit me," Antony would later say. "I am just a man."

[14]From a personal interview with Very Rev. Joseph Shaheen.

The greatness of Antony Bashir was because of his humanity, not in spite of it. From his humanity he learned humility. Because of his humanity, his clergy knew he was approachable, and they drew close to him.[15]

Reminiscences of Fr Louie Mahshe

Antony Bashir was a genius of a man who believed in sheer excellence, in himself, and in his faith. He would say to a priest he was about to ordain, "No matter how inadequate you feel you are, don't worry, son. God knows how inadequate we all are for the office. Believe in yourself, and believe in our God. The office will make you into the man you are supposed to be. You must become the man that the office will make of you."

During the Great Depression years of the thirties, President Franklin Roosevelt said, "The only thing we have to fear is fear itself." Antony understood those words well. He knew that fear created a paralysis. He knew that his immigrant clergy needed to overcome their fear. Antony knew that God would grow them if they would do their part. He motivated them to become the men that God had called them to be. He inspired confidence and courage, but it was a confidence and courage tempered with humility, not arrogance. Antony knew that if his priests were not afraid, they could inspire their people also to not be afraid.

Antony also knew that the archdiocese, for whose undivided life he so fiercely fought, had not yet become all that it could be. In his dying days, he said time and time again, "For God's sake, do not let anyone divide you."[16]

Reminiscences of Fr Antony Gabriel

I remember when I was nine years old. We lived in Syracuse, New York. We used to host a large *mahrajyan*. Antony was a nice man. He insisted that the congregation invite Samuel David. After the Divine

[15]From a personal interview with Very Rev. John Badeen.
[16]From a personal interview with Rev. Louie Mahshe.

Liturgy was celebrated in church, they would take him to the *mahra-jyan* in an open car. He used to put me on his lap. He was close to my family. On the way he would ask Samuel David to sing. David would sing "My Country 'Tis of Thee," "God Bless America," "It is truly meet," and other songs. His voice was beautiful and loud. When he would stop singing, Antony would clap his hands and ask him to sing some more. He had a great capacity for love. He had great humility. There was a sense of greatness about him.

My given name was Kenneth Gabriel. Years later, when I was ordained, he said to me, "Kenneth, what would you like to be called?" I replied, "I think I would like to be called Elias." When the day for my ordination came, His Eminence ordained me "Antony." I was shaken when he said his name on my head. He said, "You are my namesake and my son. I expect great things from you."

I never forgot those words. In the same liturgy, he said, "Where there is a will, there is a way. Nothing can stop you from accomplishing anything in this life." Later, I came home and wrote those words in all my books. Those words encouraged me, challenged me, and inspired me to further my education, to go to graduate school, and to write. Think about it. Someone coming from my background would never think of dreaming of doing such things. But he planted the idea in me that a person can be great by exercising his will.

I used to travel with Antony Bashir when I was at the seminary. We would have long talks. I learned so much from him. He was tall in height, but his heart was as large as he was tall. In spite of his greatness, he had a great sense of humility.

I will never forget that I drove him to St Nicholas Cathedral in Brooklyn, New York. He went before Archimandrite Ananias Kassab, knelt, and took confession. I don't think anyone ever saw him do that. Afterward, I said to him, "Saidna, I saw you taking confession." He said, "There is no one who is so great that he can't kneel before God and ask forgiveness for his sins."

Once I went with Bashir to Bridgeport, Connecticut. The community gave me a $100 scholarship, which went a long way in 1958. He grasped it out of my hand and said, "I'll take care of it." I said, "Saidna, is that check for me?" He replied, "We'll see."

When I got back to the seminary, I bought a set of books of the Church Fathers and sent the bill to him. When he received the bill he called and said, "For God's sake, why did you send me this bill?" I told him, "You got the $100 gift which was given to me for a scholarship. So you got the check, and I got the books." He laughed and said, "You're the first one ever to get any money out of me."

I still have the books, and I keep them in memory of him. We collected money for a briefcase for him, and we took it to him for Christmas. Aunt Adele said, "Why did you spend money on him?" At his funeral, she brought the briefcase and said, "You take this briefcase in memory of his blessed soul." She kept it with her all this time, but she wanted to give it to me for his memory.

Abdallah Khoury was a member of the Archdiocese Board of Trustees. The archdiocese sent gospel books to the churches in the old country; they were paid for by Mr Khoury. Bashir, in his eulogy for Khoury, recalled: "Abdallah Khoury told me, 'Bashir, you must work and conquer and break the bones of those who reject the gospel and unity, just like you break a watermelon.'"

He would use Khalil Gibran and Elia Abu Madi in his messages. He was inspired by the philosophy of Khalil Gibran, Abdul Haddad, and Mikhael Neiemy. I used to analyze his sermons just as I did his eulogy of Abdallah Khoury, which I could listen to over and over again. He was very much influenced by these literary giants. One thing that he said struck me at the time: "Abdallah Khoury's soul has flown like a dove to heaven." He knew how to use poetic language. I still have the recording.

Antony mingled literary giants with the Scriptures. He spoke on the Scriptures when it was necessary, but he used practical philosophy. All you have to do is follow his messages in *The Word* magazine to the clergy and you can see why Alexander Schmemann called him a "practical theologian and the father of American Orthodoxy." He took his theology and brought it to the common person so they could understand it.

Think of it. The man walked with presidents one day, and the next day he was at a *mahrajyan* clapping and cheering his flock, and with the regular people the next weekend. His sermons were always peppered with folksy stuff from Lebanon and from Arabic writers. He used the common knowledge that was the context of his time to connect with the common people.

I must have a million stories about Antony Bashir. For me, he epitomized the man from Douma who achieved greatness by building the Church in North America. He stood among many great giants who served the Church. When he was lying in his coffin, Protosyngellos Ellis Khoury was standing next to me as prayers were being read and many, many bishops and priests passed by with long beards and flowing robes. Ellis Khoury commented to me, "Even in death he stands greater than those who surrounded him in life; his shadow looms so large."

And so I carry his name. It is a badge of honor for me. I think that as long as I live, I will be ever grateful for the huge lessons in life he imparted to our generation of priests. I am sorry that so many will never have the opportunity to touch the hem of a man as great as Antony Bashir. He epitomized what Khalil Gibran once wrote, that "work is love made manifest." He was close to the poet Elia Abou Madi, who gave a eulogy most outstanding. He said that one plants a seed that bears fruit in the hearts of those you leave behind. Antony Bashir was a gentle giant who left seeds behind in our hearts. Some people think that he was very secular, but for me, he was a twentieth-century saint, because he sacrificed all his life. When I hear people criticize him, I get away from them.

His is a great legacy. I know people say he was tight. But I see him like those that came from the old country with nothing and put away for the next generation. He laid a marvelous foundation of growth. His successor, Metropolitan Philip Saliba, has accomplished great things by building on the foundation laid by Antony Bashir.[17]

Final Reminiscences of Fr Joseph Shaheen

Bashir adopted each one of us as his sons. We were far from being contemporaries, but he adopted and trusted us as sons, emotionally and

[17]From a personal interview with Very Rev. Antony Gabriel.

financially. Like his children, he would discipline us in a very fatherly manner, if we were out of line. He would let us know that he would not put up with any nonsense. I felt in this his fatherly character. At his funeral, I stared at him. I was thinking of the prayer, "your father in God." I really felt that I had lost my father.[18]

The Author's Personal Memories

In the summer of 1961, after celebrating the Divine Liturgy at St Thomas Church in Sioux City, Iowa, Metropolitan Antony came to St Mary's in Omaha, Nebraska, where my father was the priest. He came to celebrate the *Artoklasia*, the blessing of the five loaves. He was accompanied by Mr Farris of the Archdiocese Board of Trustees. I had heard about him, but had never met him. He was a tall, bald-headed man. Of course, everyone in our small community was eager to welcome him and to receive his blessing. I served as an altar boy during the service. Inside the altar, Philip Abdouch gave me the basket of bread to take outside and hold for His Eminence. As the people came forward to reverence the cross, Metropolitan Antony gave each a piece of the bread from the basket I was holding.

At the end of the service, Metropolitan Antony returned to the altar area, as did I. It was then that it dawned on me that I had not received my blessing and my piece of bread. I went to him, held out my cupped hands, and asked, "Will you bless me?" He shook his finger at me, and said sternly in a deep voice, "Who do you think you are, a priest's son? You take your blessing outside like everyone else. Priest's sons have no privileges." I was shaking as I went outside, and he came out and blessed me. For many, many years, when anyone said the name "Antony Bashir," a cloud of fear and trembling would come over me.

A second memory I have took place in 1963. My father was transferred to St George in Albany, New York. Out of respect he made an appointment to visit His Eminence at his office in Bayridge. My father took me with him on the bus. We left early in the morning and arrived

[18]From a personal interview with Rev. Joseph Shaheen.

at New York Central Station around noon. My father inquired on how to get to Bayridge. On our way to Bayridge, I told my dad, "I'm hungry; let's get something to eat." Dad said, "No, the Metropolitan is preparing lunch for us, so we must hurry."

When we got there, his sister Adele opened the door and welcomed us. My father went inside the metropolitan's office, and I waited in the foyer. Time passed. My stomach was growling. Adele gave me a glass of grape juice to drink. Later, I was called in to the metropolitan's office. I saw that my dad had a cup of coffee. I think my father was hopeful that I would enter the priesthood and that this visit would help. His Eminence told me to finish college and then come see him again. We went out to the foyer where the Metropolitan smoked a cigar. After an hour and a half, we left. My dad and I were starving. We quickly found a restaurant around the corner and got something to eat. Maybe he thought we'd already eaten. I don't know. But he did not ask us whether we had eaten. Maybe it was his way of saving money.

Summary

Metropolitan Antony was quite a contradictory character. He supported the mother church of Antioch, the clergy, and the seminarians. Yet, if he could get a penny from you, he would. If he was able to get a suit from a factory, he would. He labored to save even a dime for the church. And whatever he saved, he left to the archdiocese. Three days before his passing, he informed Monsour Laham where the money had been invested. He did not hire a secretary or a cook. His sister Adele lived with him and took care of his necessities. All his correspondence was typed by himself, having his own typewriter in English and in Arabic. He typed like my father Zacharia, with one finger. One wonders how he accomplished all he did.

Antony had a very deep voice. When I think of him, I find myself standing before him at St Mary in Omaha, Nebraska, and I can still hear that deep, scratchy voice. Many tried to mimic him, just to recall the past of this great man, a giant among men. But Antony faced pain and personal challenges like everyone else. One may think that, because he was a bishop, he was immune from the problems of health. He kept his health condition to himself, believing that he would overcome his sickness. Philip Haddad remembered him at a convention, sitting next to him. "He was shaking his legs and I said, 'What are you doing?' He said, 'I just had a hemorrhoid operation. I don't feel good.' It was very rare that he complained about his health."[19]

Antony's life was the Church and her well-being in this land. He fostered and labored for unity and planned for the challenges that were about to face the Church. As John Dalack said, "He is the one who put us on his shoulders, so to speak, and once we were on his shoulders there was a lot we could see and do. He put us in a position that we could achieve what has been achieved. By putting us on his shoulders we were able to see much more than he could see. He was the person we needed for the time. What he was able to do for the Church needed to be done."[20]

[19]Haddad, personal interview
[20]Dalack, personal interview

CHAPTER 15

A Lasting Legacy

I t is not an exaggeration to call Metropolitan Antony Bashir the
founder of the Antiochian Archdiocese of New York and all North
America. A lesser man would have surrendered in the face of the
interference that came from the Holy Synod of Antioch, interference
that continued to exacerbate the problems with the Toledo group. His
singular commitment to the unity of the Church among Antiochians
in America instilled a commitment to unity into the very ethos of the
archdiocese. Because of Antony, unity within the archdiocese is a con-
crete reality.

Administrative Founder

Because of Bashir's experience with Episcopalian conventions when
he first arrived in the United States, "the Antiochians were the first
[Orthodox] in North America to establish the system of Archdiocese
conventions. The first was in 1937. The second was in 1947 and there-
after on an annual basis, until changed under Metropolitan Philip's
primacy to biennial events."[1]

Under Antony's leadership, SOYO, which began locally in New
England in 1938, eventually became a national movement and spread
throughout North American. "Its primary motivation was to knit
together the fragmented youth groups in the United States and
Canada."[2] The regional SOYO conventions helped to re-energize the
parish on the local level.

[1] Antony Gabriel, "Lest We Forget," 5.
[2] Ibid., 6.

Antony led the archdiocese in the creation of parish councils or boards, governed by constitutions and by-laws, which helped administer the local parishes. He also led the archdiocese in the creation of a variety of departments and commissions that "addressed the pressing needs of the archdiocese—many of which are still active and thriving."[3]

When he would visit a parish in the early years of his ministry, Bashir would collect a *nourieh*, or stipend, for the clergy by going from door-to-door. He used to tell seminarians that they had be God's salesman, and had to have the "ability to sell religion to the parishioners as one would sell plots of land on Lake Erie."[4] The concept of tithing, as practiced by most Protestant churches in America, was virtually unknown in "the old countries." So Antony evolved the *nourieh* into a head tax known as the "parish assessment." When it started, each parish paid to the archdiocese one dollar for each baptized soul in the parish. This was designed to "ensure fiscal security for the Archdiocese."[5] This assessment system would serve the archdiocese for decades, until, under Metropolitan Philip, it was replaced by a system of parish tithes.

Under Bashir, the archdiocese continued to grow. In 1960, he inaugurated a system of deaneries to assist him in his pastoral and administrative work. And though he may have felt rather ambivalent himself about having auxiliary bishops, he was nonetheless the one who set in motion the process that would eventually result in the appointment of other bishops to assist the metropolitan.[6]

According to Fr Antony Gabriel, while Bashir at first administered his diocese alone, he was able to change when the need arose.

He ultimately possessed the genius which listened to the advice of his faithful lieutenants. He knew instinctively he had to share the administration of the archdiocese as it expanded, particularly with the young men returning home from the horrors of the war [World

[3]Ibid., 7.
[4]Ibid., 5.
[5]Ibid., 8.
[6]Ibid., 12.

War II], and for whom the Church remained a safe haven and bastion of community solidarity. Without the organized institution of the archdiocese and subsidiary organizations, he could not sustain the loyalty of the new generation of Antiochians.[7]

Creating a Controversy

Antony Bashir believed in the unity of the Church, and he embraced gladly the winds of ecumenical dialogue that blew in the twentieth century, seeking the reunion of Christendom. "He . . . was in the vanguard as a supporter of the urgent necessity for a united front against . . . the assault on Christianity by communism and secularism."[8] His thinking on ecumenism was shaped by his participation in the Episcopal General Convention in 1922 and the Edinburgh/Oxford Conference in 1938, and the statement on Protestant Episcopal ministrations that was first issued by Bishop Raphael in 1912, affirmed by Aftimios in 1927, and reaffirmed by Antony in 1944.

On January 26, 1958, at St Mary Church in Brooklyn, New York, Metropolitan Antony Bashir made the momentous pronouncement introducing an Orthodox Western Rite.[9] He established a Western Rite Vicariate under Alexander Turner. This act caused considerable controversy, especially in the theological academies. "He used the 1958 encyclical of Patriarch Alexander III as the *raison d'être* for this bold stroke."[10] Fr Alexander Schmemann, dean of St Vladimir's Seminary, was quick to respond to Antony's edict by publishing his objections in the St Vladimir's Seminary Quarterly.[11]

[7]Ibid., 5.
[8]Ibid., 10.
[9]*The Word* 2. 8 (August 1958): 21.
[10]Antony Gabriel, 'Lest We Forget,' 12.
[11]Alexander Schmemann, 'The Western Rite,' *St. Vladimir's Seminary Quarterly,* 2. 4 (Fall 1958): 37–38; and Alexander Schmemann, 'III. Some Reflections upon 'A Case Study," *St. Vladimir's Seminary Quarterly,* 24. 4 (1980): 266–269.

Founder of the American Orthodox Church

In an era when the bright lights of the promised land of America had given way to homesickness, nostalgia ran rampant among the immigrants. Local parishes became ethnic community centers. Antony Bashir, fully eastern in his Christianity, stood fully westward culturally. He caused his Church to look westward. He put his hands to the plow in this land and did not look backwards to a former land. Indeed, unlike Lot's wife, and many other bishops, he refused to look back. "He used his God-given intellectual and spiritual talents to immerse himself in his adopted country and culture. He incorporated in his person and acts what he perceived to be 'useful' from the wellspring of Orthodoxy and married them to Western moralities."[12]

Antony Bashir thoroughly committed himself to planting and building an American Orthodox Church. In 1957, he delivered an address to a meeting of the Council of Churches, in which he declared:

> Orthodoxy is a freedom-loving, democratic faith . . . it is at its best in our free America. Our people are part and parcel of America, gladly giving their treasure and the blood of their sons to safeguard its free institutions which are the reflection of the freedom they find in their faith. If the best of Byzantium has survived, it is in the United States, and if there is an Orthodox political ideal, it is enshrined in the Constitution and Declaration of Independence.[13]

Antony understood that the Orthodox churches in America were still immigrant churches. But he refused to allow the Antiochian Church to become a ghetto church, little more than outposts of "the old country." He actively sought to "Americanize" his immigrant Church.

> Thus while we must still minister to many who remember the ways and customs of another land, it is our policy to make our Church in the United States an American Church. In my own archdiocese, under my administration, we have pioneered the intro-

---

[12]Ibid.

[13]Antony Bashir, cited in Antony Gabriel, 'Lest We Forget,' 1.

duction of English service books and the training of English-speaking priests. We are tied to no sacred language; we recognize all tongues as the creation of God, and employ them in His worship. We have no desire to perpetuate anything but the Gospel of Christ, and that we can do as effectively in English as in any other tongue.[14]

It was his unflinching commitment to perpetuating the gospel in America that caused Fr Alexander Schmemann to say that "in the history of the Church here, in the kind of spiritual iconostasis of the American Church, he certainly would be the *Founding Father of the American Orthodox Church.*"[15]

Furthermore, his years of being betrayed by the Holy Synod overseas with regard to the Toledo problem caused him to embrace even more boldly the planting and creating of an American Orthodox Church, free of Old World politics and alive with democratic freedom.

> He had no illusions about the possibility of the Church here being governed from abroad; no illusions whatsoever. He knew it was impossible; he gave up on diplomacy with the old country long ago. I think when history is finally written, and we see him in his true perspective, I think that of all the bishops of this particular era, he was, more than all the Russian bishops, great in his vision, and was therefore a real father of American Orthodoxy. He is much more a founding father than Leonty, because he and the others were thoroughly Russian. He, being a thorough Arab, still knew already that the center is here and nowhere else. This is the most important point about him. He inspired people with the call to be an American Orthodox Church.[16]

Bold Enough To Question American Foreign Policy

Antony Bashir was an American, but he was not blind to what he thought wrong in America. In his public remarks at the 1948 Arch-

[14]Ibid.
[15]Schmemann, personal interview. Italics mine.
[16]Ibid.

diocesan Convention, he became the first hierarch to attack the policy of the United States government in supporting the creation of Israel. He protested the treatment of the Palestinian peoples and foresaw that there would be unsettling conditions and no peace in the region as a result. In 1957, he remarked that "the main cause of the Middle East problem is the presence of one million miserable, desperate Arab refugees, and there will never be peace as long as the refugees remain. It is the duty of the Christian world to do something about it."[17]

He Laid a Foundation

> According to the grace of God which was given to me, as a wise master builder I laid a foundation.
>
> 1 Corinthians 3:10

Metropolitan Antony Bashir led the Antiochian Archdiocese for thirty years with a singular vision of unity. He believed in the unity of the Antiochian Archdiocese and labored tirelessly against forces in Toledo and in the Holy Synod that sought to destroy that unity. Much of his life was wasted in dealing with the fickleness of the Holy Synod. Yet his disappointments in dealing with "the old country," as we said above, only sharpened his resolve to embrace the American spirit of freedom.

He believed in the unity of the whole Orthodox Church in America. He actively recruited bishops and leaders within other Orthodox jurisdictions to turn away from their own "old countries" and embrace the planting and creating of an American Orthodox Church in North America. He did not live to see the unity of Toledo with the Antiochian Archdiocese. But, thankfully, that day did finally come. Sadly, the dream of a united American Orthodox Church remains just that, a dream. Yet that dream continues to burn brightly within the Antiochian Archdiocese. Metropolitan Philip took up the call for the unity of the Archdiocese with Toledo and achieved it. He has also been

---

[17]see Antony Gabriel, 'Lest We Forget,' 13.

a leading voice in his generation urging and prodding fellow hierarchs to embrace the unity of a single Orthodox Church in America.

St Paul said that, as a wise master builder, he had laid a foundation that another was now building upon. He admonished those who followed him to be careful how they built upon that foundation. It is a great testimony to Bashir's leadership and vision to see that his foundation was solid and could be built upon. It was neither abandoned nor razed to the ground. The great things that have been accomplished during Metropolitan Philip's tenure could not have been achieved without that firm foundation upon which they are built, a foundation laid by Antony Bashir.

A Final Word

Metropolitan Antony was a direct and outspoken spiritual father. He believed in the Orthodox Church and its teachings, and he welcomed all who wanted to enter the Orthodox Church. He believed in the unity of Christendom throughout the world. His life and actions demonstrated that he lived what he prayed: "for the peace of the whole world, for the good estate of the holy churches of God, and for the union of all men."

He embraced the fresh air of North America. He did not look backwards to the Middle East whence he came. He embraced the true missionary spirit of the Church of Antioch that had sent forth Ss Paul and Barnabas on the first missionary journey. He embraced the Apostolic Council held in Jerusalem in the Book of Acts that decided converts did not need to become Jews to be Christians. Antony did not believe that people had to become Russians or Greeks or Arabs in order to embrace the Orthodox faith. He embraced America by embracing the English language. Americans did not have to learn Russian, or Greek, or Arabic in order to become Orthodox. In the true spirit of Pentecost, because of Metropolitan Antony's ministry, Americans could hear the gospel in their own language.

He knew that the immigrant generation would give way to succeeding generations born in North America. He knew that the Church in America must speak the language of America—not just English, but also the "languages" of business, finance, and democracy that spring from the self-evident ideals within American culture. Someday, when Orthodox unity is achieved in America, it will have been achieved because others have chosen to breathe the same American air that Antony Bashir breathed and have allowed the same spirit of the gospel that animated his life and ministry to animate and empower their lives and ministries. When that day comes, those who have taken their stand with him will acknowledge Antony Bashir as one of the founding fathers of the American Orthodox Church. May his memory be eternal.

Selected Bibliography

Aboud, Gregory. *The Syrian Antiochian Orthodox Church of America.* Unpublished manuscript, 1962.

Anonymous. *Journal of the General Convention of the Protestant Episcopal Church.* Portland, Oregon: 1922.

Anonymous. "The Self-Ruled Antiochian Orthodox Christian Archdiocese of North America: A Brief History." *The Self-Ruled Antiochian Orthodox Christian Archdiocese of North America 2011 Directory* (Englewood, NJ: 2011): 1–6.

Gabriel, Antony. "A Man to Match the Mountains." *The 25th Antiochian Orthodox Archdiocese Convention.* Chicago, IL: 1970.

Gabriel, Antony. *The Ancient Church on New Shores: Antioch in North America.* San Bernardino, CA: St. Willibord's Press, 1996.

Gabriel, Antony. "Lest We Forget: The Administrative Legacy of Antony Bashir (1936–1966)." Unpublished article, July 1997.

Gibran, Khalil. *Tolstoy's Confession and His Philosophy* (Arabic edition). Antony Bashir, trans. Cairo: Elias' Modern Press, 1932.

Ham, Herb. *The Immigrant's Tale: A Cultural History of Eastern Orthodox Christianity's 20th Century Migration to the United States.* Unpublished manuscript.

Hyder, Charles T. *History of New England S.O.Y.O.* Lawrence, MA: 1963.

Kafoure, William G. *S.O.Y.O Digest* 5.1 (March 1955).

Kafoure, William G. *S.O.Y.O. Digest* 5. 4 (December 1955).

Karbawey, Basil. *The New Herodus.* USA: 1925.

Nahas, Nicholaos. *The Witness of Antioch in North America.*

Ofiesh, Aftimios. *The Orthodox Catholic Review* 1. 2 (February 1927).

Ofiesh, Aftimios. *The Orthodox Catholic Review* 1. 4–5 (April-May 1927).

Ofiesh, Mariam Namey. *Archbishop Aftimios Ofiesh.* Sun City West, AZ: Aftimios Abihider, 1999.

Rados, George M. *St. George Orthodox Church: 40th Anniversary.* Terre Haute, ID: 1967.

Schmemann, Alexander. "The Western Rite." *St. Vladimir's Seminary Quarterly* 2. 4 (Fall 1958): 37–38.

_____ "III. Some Reflections upon 'A Case Study.' " *St. Vladimir's Seminary Quarterly* 24. 4 (1980): 266–269.

Salem, Sam E. *Metropolitan Antony Bashir: An Appreciation.* Cleveland, OH: 1961.

Upson, Stephen. "History of the Antiochian Orthodox Christian Archdiocese of All New York and North America." *The 25th Antiochian Orthodox Archdiocese Convention.* Chicago:1970.

Zibrinskie, George. *Orthodox American Church.* 1928

St Vladimir's Theological Quarterly 5 (1961)

Time Magazine (May 4, 1936)

The Word 1. 2 (February 1957)

_____ 1.1 (January 1957)

_____ 2. 8 (August 1958)

_____ 2.10 (October 1958)

_____ 2. 11 (November 1958)

_____ 2.12 (December 1958)

_____ 3. 7 (September 1959)

_____ 3. 9 (November 1959)

_____ 4. 2 (February 1960)

_____ 4. 7 (September 1960)

_____ 6. 1 (January 1962)

_____ 6. 3 (March 1962)

_____ 6. 9 (September 1962)

_____ 6. 10 (October 1962)

_____ 6. 11 (November 1962)

_____ 10. 3 (March 1966)

_____ 10. 4–5 (April-May 1966)

_____ 10. 6–7 (June-September 1966)

_____ 15. 10 (December 1971)